# STYLE
## AND THE
## SUCCESSFUL
## GIRL

Successful Girls always have style!

# STYLE
# AND THE
# SUCCESSFUL
# GIRL

**Transform Your Look, Transform Your Life**

## GRETTA MONAHAN

**Foreword by Rachael Ray**

GOTHAM
BOOKS

GOTHAM
BOOKS

GOTHAM BOOKS

Published by the Penguin Group

Penguin Group (USA), 375 Hudson Street,

New York, New York 10014, USA

USA / Canada / UK / Ireland / Australia / New Zealand / India / South Africa / China

Penguin Books Ltd, Registered Offices: 80 Strand, London WC2R 0RL, England

For more information about the Penguin Group visit penguin.com.

LIBRARY OF CONGRESS CATALOGING-IN-PUBLICATION DATA
has been applied for.

ISBN 978-1-592-40794-1

Printed in the United States of America

1  3  5  7  9  10  8  6  4  2

Set in Bodoni and Benton Sans.

Designed by Vertigo Design NYC

Produced by Stonesong www.stonesong.com

I dedicate this book in loving memory to the original
Successful Girl of my life, my beloved Aunt Kathy
whose love, strength, lessons, and spirit continue
to guide and inspire me . . . we did it!

# CONTENTS

# FOREWORD

**MY BRAND IS ABOUT THE MOTTO CAN DO!**
I consider a large part of my job to be giving our viewers and readers a chance to share in everything they see on our TV shows or in print, whether that be a recipe or ideas on fashion or lifestyle. We want those watching or reading to be successful with the advice or information we share with them. On my daytime TV show and in our magazine, *Every Day*, Gretta Monahan has become a style guru that we can all trust. (I nicknamed Gretta "G" because she is so Money!) Gretta's imaginative and affordable jaw-dropping beauty and fashion makeovers have been a beyond-the-kitchen signature segment of the show for seven seasons, and we look forward to those yet to come.

Cooking is a self-esteem builder because it is immediate —taking raw ingredients and making something delicious feeds the soul. We all want that same boost to our self-esteem when we leave our kitchens and look in the mirror. As women, we so often put ourselves last, and we need someone like Gretta to help us feel a little saucier and more delicious in our day-to-day lifestyle. I enjoy watching Gretta's amazing transformations because she performs so many of them not on models but on our

# by RACHAEL RAY

actual viewers and readers, and the changes are more than superficial. Once the show is over the take-home benefits keep going. Participants and viewers say Gretta's beauty and style tips empower them to make even bigger life changes—get a new job, improve their relationship or find a better one, recover their self-esteem and mojo, and most of all, move forward when they've felt stuck in a rut.

If your closet is a mash-up of mistakes, your body and clothes have nothing in common, and you spend more time on beauty routines than living life, grab a copy of *Style and The Successful Girl*! This book will help you recognize and define your style, sharpen your shopping and beauty skills, and teach you everything you need to know to get more bang for your buck and your time. By the time you're done reading you'll know which ingredients make up your recipe for looking your best.

— *Rachael Ray*

*We all want that same boost to our self-esteem when we leave our kitchens and look in the mirror.*

# MY OWN SUCCESS STORY

**MY APPROACH TO STYLE AND BEAUTY** is really similar to how Rachael Ray works with food. We both take everyday ingredients and put them together in an easy recipe that guarantees success. You probably have a lot of clothes, makeup, and hair "ingredients" at home now, but here's the catch: Some of them are stale, can't satisfy your style cravings, and don't provide a reliable menu of options for your multitasking, 24/7 lifestyle.

I'm not going to preach unrealistic rules. You don't need to wear a size two, have a lot of money or a perfect body, be able to afford a designer wardrobe, be a certain age, go to fancy salons and spas, or live in New York, Paris, or Milan to be a Successful Girl with Style.

FYI, like most of you I'm no longer a "girl." But all women keep that girl spirit no matter what our true age. It's what keeps us up, sexy, and fun with an adventurous attitude and willingness to keep growing, evolving, and learning.

*Style and the Successful Girl* is every girl's fashion and beauty blueprint to navigating the ups and downs of our lifestyles, jobs, age, body changes, and relationships. You'll discover the successful strategies and techniques I've developed and continue to use as a stylist on my clients —both real women and celebs.

Let's start with my story. You may have a similar one or recognize some of my situations as I've-been-there-too moments. Raised in Boston by divorced parents, including a mom with serious medical issues, I had no siblings to bond with and certainly no fashion pedigree. Basically, I was a tomboy-meets-wanna-be-princess. My life changed when I discovered fashion magazines after school at the library. By eighth grade, I was living with my aunt Kathy, and life became a tutorial in how to wear false lashes, perfume, jewelry, and fabulous clothes. She became my first style guru and

> *I'm not going to preach unrealistic rules.*

role model. Aunt Kathy was the first successful working woman in my family who was financially independent and stylish. Aside from her strong work ethic, my aunt had a strategy for taking care of her looks. My friends' moms didn't do aerobics, get facials, take vitamins, or know everything about accessorizing, but Aunt Kathy opened a door to a world that instantly felt like home.

My best friend, Brenda, was a young Heather Locklear–type. After a day window-shopping at the mall, we'd return home to experiment with our own jeans, hair, and makeup. Sometimes our DIY projects were home runs, and sometimes they were disasters—like my orange Sun-In hair and crispy perm. I loved all of it anyway and caught a serious fashion bug.

Gramma Kay and mom

My stylish mom

Me with Aunt Kathy at her exercise class

My gorgeous grandmother Kay

By age seventeen, I was enrolled at FIT (Fashion Institute of Technology) in NYC as a fashion design student. I spent evenings sewing labels on garments to support myself. Sometimes I worked as a gofer for a hair and makeup artist on magazine shoots. Mainly my job was getting coffee and cleaning her brushes. One day she asked me to step in and get hair and makeup started on some of the models. Beauty became my new focus. I left NYC and returned to Boston to attend cosmetology/hairdressing school at night while working as a counter makeup artist during the day. In class I met "Nicole," who became a friend and eventually my business partner. At the age of twenty-four, I opened my own salon; at twenty-six, I added a spa; and by thirty-one, I had started my first high-end fashion boutique. Ten years from my starting date, I owned a salon/spa/retail empire that exceeded ten million dollars. Running multiple businesses simultaneously taught me to multitask, and I incorporate this philosophy into every area of my life—including my fashion and beauty strategy. Now, as a style expert and businesswoman with a family life and son, Kai Rei, looking good 24/7 is my only option!

Not bad for a kid who started out with nothing but imagination and guts. I continued to grow, and as a graduate of Harvard Business School's Owner/President/Management program I had more than a decade of retail and management experience under my Prada belt.

Going to the runway shows in New York, Paris, and Milan gives me a chance to get the inside scoop on trends and people-watch at the same time. But what makes me happiest is helping real, everyday women turn their stuck-in-a-rut stories into success. As a style expert on *Every Day with Rachael Ray* and other shows—I cohosted the second season of Tim Gunn's *Guide to Style* on Bravo and have been a contributor on *Live With Kelly and Michael*, *The View*, *Good Morning America*, and *Today*—I get to do exactly that. My own multitasking lifestyle keeps me on my toes, and my tips work because I live them!

*Together we can make this year your most successful!*
*Can't wait to get started!*

# IN STYLE AND THE SUCCESSFUL GIRL YOU'LL LEARN

**How to find your very own iconic style.**

My DIY system determines which look—weekend, girly, sophisticated, or sexy—is you. It's going to change the way you shop and dress forever.

**How to use successful style to get what you want.**

We all have individual goals. If you want to shop smarter, move up the ladder at work, find the right relationship, get your clothes and body in sync, or manage pregnancy without losing a beat, my tips and tricks will guarantee your goals.

**How to self-diagnose your problem zones and solve the issues.**

The #1 obstacle to success is not being sure where you need help, why, and what to do about it. Find your true body silhouette, and use it to style up.

**What's really sabotaging your success and how to move on.**

Girls who are stuck in a style rut often keep repeating the same style mistakes. Learn what works for you and how to stay consistent while you keep updating and evolving with trends.

**How to know where to start and when to stop.**

Rarely does any girl need a head-to-toe makeover. Sometimes a small change is the one that makes the biggest difference between failure and success.

**How to make your "ingredients" into a delicious fashion soup.**

A lot of what you own is better than you thought. Learn to dish it up in a new way. Success is all in the mix, proportions, and technique.

**Which gotta-have items do you need?**

Success 24/7 is easy if you always keep these in mind. My go-tos are heels, lash extensions, and accessories; yours might be fitted jeans, a leather jacket, and bangs, or a dress, red lipstick, and a big, fabulous bag.

# CHAPTER 1

# FAKE IT TILL YOU MAKE IT

*T*HE SUCCESSFUL GIRL always wears clothes she loves that love her back. I think finding your best look is a lot like matchmaking. We're hopeless romantics about relationships and style. We wonder if our clothes crushes and fashion flings will disappoint or promise to love us forever. If our closets are any indication, we've had a lot of bad dates, creepy fix-ups, and a few unexpected break-ups when it comes to style. Fifty percent of our wardrobe is probably "unsuccessful" because the items were a bad match from the minute we plunked down the plastic card. What are we missing, and where are we messing up? Every woman wants the "sure," confident feeling that knowing exactly what to wear and how to put it all together provides. Making it means you have finally found your perfect formula for successful style. Until then you've simply got to fake it, and I'll show you how.

First, think about fashion icons or friends who always get their style right, and you'll notice a consistent thread running through every look. Their personal style is identifiable no matter what they're wearing or what the season or situation is. They stick to their look and never let fashion trends control their clothes. Of course, they pay attention to trends, but they find a way to incorporate them without being slaves to the runway or changing who they are. They have found their perfect match. What's their secret? Truthfully, some women just have an inborn knack or had a good style role model early on in life, but the rest of us can learn that skill too. By the time you read the last page of *Style and the Successful Girl*, you'll have graduated from faking it to making it. You'll be your own best stylist with a wardrobe that's a genuine ally, and you'll avoid making fashion and beauty mistakes that are roadblocks to success.

Personal style doesn't happen overnight despite the inspirational makeovers you see on TV, in magazines, or in advice books like this one. Before-and-after photos look magical, and they do lift the participant out of a fashion rut. The real benefit is the ripple reaction that encourages viewers and readers to change. Before-and-afters are contagious! I realize most women will never have the opportunity for a do-over with an A-list pro team, but that's OK for two reasons. The first is that learning to trust your own taste, needs, and style is the key to really developing your own

> *Finding your optimum look is a process, not a one-thing-works-for-all formula.*

iconic look. You'll be your own ace expert and know precisely what to look for and what to reject as "not me." The second reason is that very rarely does anyone truly need a head-to-toe change. I've seen major, OMG style moments happen though one small change. Maybe you realize dresses flatter you most and simplify your life by eliminating the need to match tops and bottoms every day. Maybe after years of covering up your curves you discover that your small waist is an asset and make belts your new best friend. Instead of hiding under layers, you start defining everything from coats to jackets and cardigans. Small things, big change.

Finding your optimum look is a process, not a one-thing-works-for-all formula. Think of yourself as the CEO in charge of creating the blueprint for your successful style. As with any smart business plan, you'll need research, a multistep strategy, and a realistic attitude.

# THE GOTTA-HAVES

BEGIN BY FAKING IT WITH A STARTER KIT OF TEN LOVE-YOU-BACK CLOTHES AND ACCESSORIES. THESE ARE YOUR FASHION SOUL MATES. THEY'RE HARDWORKING, EVERYDAY, BASIC FASHION INGREDIENTS YOU ALREADY OWN, LIKE THE DARK JEANS THAT MAKE YOU FEEL SKINNY AND NEVER LET YOU DOWN. THEY'RE ROCK STEADY AND ALWAYS READY WITH UNCONDITIONAL FLATTERY. THESE CLOTHES MAY NOT HAVE FASHION EDITORS AND BLOGGERS JUMPING OUT OF THEIR SEATS, BUT THEY MAKE YOU FEEL SEXY, GLAMOROUS, CONFIDENT, AND RELAXED.

## This is your starter kit for success

You may be tempted by trends and fancy fads, but these ten things are the ones you keep going back to again and again. Every time you slip into "bad-fashion-day" mode, they save you. Best of all, you can count on them to consistently reap compliments. Maybe it's the tailored jacket that makes you look like an exec and the four-inch heels that make you strut like Giselle. Maybe it's the faux diamond hoops that make you sparkle and the red shift dress that makes everyone say, "You look great! Did you lose weight?!" Maybe it's the bra and your secret slimmer that make you say yes to a first date invite when you've got your period.

Most women have all ten basic ingredients. Some of you may even have multiples to choose from, and why not buy repeats of successful items? I'm betting you count on these pieces more frequently than you realize. They make a huge difference in the way you package and present

yourself, which is the secret to leaving a long-lasting impression and an unforgettable impact. Your top ten gotta-haves are listed on the next pages. They offer the first feel-good clues to your future style.

Ultimately, this beginner list will change, evolve, and grow, but for now the list provides a menu of options. Select à la carte for a successful ensemble right this minute. I've added a best choice in each case to help you weed through your racks and shelves. Get going! We've got a lot of work ahead, and this kit will ramp up your style power instantly.

Make these ten as basic as salt and pepper. You might even have more basic faves to add to this list like a trench, leather jacket, silk blouse, colorful cardigan, or long, drapey scarf, but use the kit as a springboard to your new look while you learn the style ropes.

# 1. A NO-FAIL LIP COLOR

Some people may not think of lip color as fashion, but it is. Lots of women apply it first thing before getting dressed for that immediate spark. Your favorite lip color dresses your face fast and pulls together any outfit—even jeans and a ponytail—with polish and power! It might be bright cherry red or shimmery caramel, a velvety plum or sheer pink, but one swipe of that no-fail lipstick/gloss/stain/tinted balm lights up your looks and smile. It makes what you say count, and that's the first step toward success. A can't-miss for chic communication with clout.

**BEST CHOICE** Go for a shade one level brighter than your natural lip color. Or . . . wear red if that's your signature.

# 2. PUMPS THAT MAKE YOUR LEGS LOOK LONGER

Slip these on and you stand up straighter, look ten pounds thinner, and walk with a supermodel swagger. They might be nude, snakeskin, or black patent, towering platforms or single-sole stilettos, peep-toes or pointy, but they do the trick every time.

**BEST CHOICE** Choose simple nude or black closed-toe pumps with a mid to high slim heel shaped to flatter your legs and with a tapered toe. FYI, curvy or muscular legs look better in stacked, contoured, or column heels (not thick, chunky, clunky ones, please), while slim legs can handle true stilettos. Look for a pair with the highest heels you can wear without complaining. The higher the heels, the more benefits for your body.

# 3. A SIGNATURE ACCESSORY

It may be a bracelet, necklace, earrings, watch, or ring, but the minute this piece of jewelry is on, you get a flash of warmth, self-assurance, and happiness. Nothing elevates what you wear and your mood more than bling. It may be fake or the real deal, a fine family heirloom like grandma's locket or something you picked up on a whim, a treat from someone special or a present to yourself.

**BEST CHOICE** Pick through your jewelry box for timeless pieces that can be worn together or independently. Mix classic and trendy, vintage and modern, fine and flea market.

# 4. DARK FITTED STRETCH JEANS

A lifestyle basic from New York to Nebraska, who can live without at least one pair of inky blue or black jeans? They do your body a huge favor by following your curves but molding them too with a hint of spandex. Nothing shakes up your mojo faster or works in seconds with any top—dressy, tailored, layered, or relaxed.

**BEST CHOICE** You want solid dark classic jeans with a medium rise and a straight, slim leg fitted to your body but not skintight. Choose a simple pair with zero embellishments and no huge logos or labels, rips, tears, big pockets, or weird seams.

## 5. THE BRA THAT MAKES YOUR BODY ROCK

It lifts your girls; smoothes out your tees, knits, and fitted tops; makes sure blouses and jackets close without pulling or gaping; and keeps all your secret sags, rolls, jiggles, and boob bloat from popping up at the wrong time and place.

**BEST CHOICE** A black or nude seamless microfiber bra with smooth cups is not negotiable. Be sure it has adjustable hooks to compensate for body fluctuations.

## 6. A LEATHER BELT THAT HELPS YOUR CURVES

A good leather belt defines your waist or hips. Loop it through your jeans or use it to cinch all your jackets, dresses, and coats. It can build up contours or make existing ones a plus.

**BEST CHOICE** A plain black leather belt one to two inches wide with a simple buckle in silver or gold (whichever metal you wear most) is essential.

## 8. A TAILORED JACKET

This power piece is pivotal to your style. It hides muffin tops and back fat, sharpens your entire silhouette, and upgrades and elevates everything from jeans to skirts and dresses. You look leaner, firmer, and gym-obsessed fit without lifting a barbell.

**BEST CHOICE** Reach for a fitted, notch-collar blazer with classic (not too wide, not too skinny) lapels in black or a dark neutral.

## 9. BOOTS

This diva-inspiring accessory makes you feel strong and powerful. Knee-high, booties, biker boots, studded, sleek, stilettos, or stacked, they make every girl feel like a wardrobe warrior.

**BEST CHOICE** Boots are so varied and personal, but you can always depend on a classic flat riding boot, knee-high boots with a heel, or booties, whichever makes you strut your stuff. This is one basic that really has three top choices.

## 7. A SHAPEWEAR BIKER SHORT THAT ERASES GUILT

Slide on this secret slimmer over pantyhose or beneath just about anything else. It flattens your tummy, firms up jiggles, and makes all your clothes fit better or just plain old fit! Even full skirts, tailored pants, and A-line dresses benefit from the holds-me-in security.

**BEST CHOICE** You may have heard it before, but a nude laser-cut bike short with a high percentage of spandex or Lycra can't be beat.

## 10. A LITTLE BRIGHT DRESS

My idea of a confidence-boosting LBD is beyond basic black; it's red or cobalt blue or an attention-getting vibrant print. It's actually a "Little Bright Dress" that adds a shot of pure style energy to your day or night.

**BEST CHOICE** A fitted sheath, straight shift, or A-line in a color that makes the most of your own hair and eye color and skin tone will work every time.

# Gretta-quette

Here's my own fake-it-till-you-make-it tale. Straight out of beauty school and wanting to start my first salon ASAP, I realized a bank loan was the answer. Big problem—I didn't have a suit and couldn't afford to splurge on an outfit to create the image of a successful, serious, but fashionable businesswoman. What I did have was a classic black pencil skirt. All I needed was a pricey-looking tailored jacket for as little money as possible. I stalked secondhand shops and found a beautiful bouclé tailored jacket. The problem? It was way too big and boxy, but the fabric was gorgeous. Thanks to my sewing skills and FIT training, I retailored it at home. That jacket and my black skirt became my breakthrough power suit. I borrowed a silk scarf and jewelry from my aunt Kathy and wore my best pumps. My VIP packaging and presentation boosted my confidence, and I got the loan!

# USE AN INSPIRATION BOARD AS A BLUEPRINT

YOUR STARTER KIT WILL TAKE THE PRESSURE OFF WHILE YOU WORK AT DEVELOPING YOUR BEST STYLE. THE SIMPLEST WAY TO DO THIS IS AT HOME WITH A CORKBOARD, PUSHPINS, AND PHOTOS OF LOOKS YOU LIKE RIPPED FROM YOUR FAVORITE MAGAZINES AND CATALOGS. MORE TECHY TYPES CAN CREATE ONLINE PHOTO MONTAGES AT SITES LIKE PINTEREST OR SHOPSTYLE.COM, BUT I LIKE THE OLD-FASHIONED TEAR-AND-TACK-UP METHOD BEST.

You can include snaps of models, celebs, and icons past and current like Audrey Hepburn, Grace Kelly, Kate Middleton, or Michelle Obama, plus photos of any accessories that catch your eye. Don't aim for organization or neat rows; just pin the snips up free form in a fashion collage. You'll soon realize the same kinds of looks attract your eye over and over. In business, this would be a creative form of information gathering, but in your case the data lead to specific patterns that identify your fashion preferences. Let the photos do the work of a consultation with a personal shopper or stylist. Your inspiration board will clarify your favorite looks right down to the details about color, jewelry, bags, and shoes. It may take days or weeks to evolve. As you add and subtract photos, you'll get closer to a real definition of how you'd like to look. Then you can start branding yourself as a woman of style because you'll finally "own" it. This is your guide to express who you are through what you wear. Study the pieces to find out why they make each look work. Determine which pieces and accessories turn up frequently and how they are put together or layered.

For example, if you see pencil skirts and cardigans showing up in several photos on your board, that's a lead. I wish I had discovered this technique years ago. It would have saved me a lot of money, time, and what-was-I-thinking moments.

## This is your guide to express who you are through what you wear.

# FIND YOUR STYLE ICONS

Basically, most inspiration boards boil down to four possible Successful Girl categories: weekend, girly, sophisticated, and sexy. Which category is the underlying theme of your favorite inspiration board? There might be some overlap, but one category will ultimately resonate with you more than the others. If you can't decide between two categories, keep working on two inspiration boards. Stick with it till one starts to jump out as the winner . . . and it will. You have met your match. Now you know why some clothes never worked for you. Take a closer look. Consider your real lifestyle and the body you currently have, but don't get too hung up on age and hair color in these inspiration boards. You'll read plenty about age and beauty in chapters 6 and 8.

Be realistic and practical about your goals. Take a good look at the photos and edit out any that don't fit your life. For example, if you're a stay-at-home mom with two small kids, a "sexy girl" inspiration board will absolutely need some adapting or rethinking! Do you really run around in minis, stilettos, and fishnets at playgroup? If you're a working mom who spends eight hours a day, five days a week in a traditional office, jeans and leggings may not be your best everyday bet. Even that category can be adapted with knits and jersey dresses. Make sure your inspiration board includes celebrities you connect to because they have the style you admire. The four "girls" listed below are the four possible style routes to success. Which one are you?

**IF YOU'RE A WEEKEND GIRL,** every day is a weekend even at work. You love jeans, leggings, ballet flats, layers of T-shirts and sweaters, knits, and anything with stretch. A lot of your clothes may be basic black pieces that fit this description. Comfort is super important to you.

**IF YOU'RE A GIRLY GIRL,** you live in dresses and skirts. You hardly ever wear pants, and when you do, they're probably jeans in pale pink. You love heels (the higher the better) and towering wedges, blouses, sweet feminine colors, small prints, florals, and ladylike details like bows, ruffles, and peplums. You don't mind a little discomfort as long as the final look makes you happy.

**IF YOU'RE A SOPHISTICATED GIRL,** your clothes are classic keepers with a contemporary spin. You love tailored pants and dresses, blazers, and structured skirts like pencils, A-lines, and pleats. You prefer luxurious fabrics and simple shapes without a lot of bells and whistles. Quality counts. You could say you're anti-trends.

**IF YOU'RE A SEXY GIRL,** your look is body-conscious and a little showy. You like to contrast tough pieces with those that are fluid and moving. You always wear lace undies and live for stilettos, fishnets, textured stockings, dangly earrings, leather, suede, fur, and animal prints.

OK! Let's start by breaking down the four iconic "girl" looks with four inspiration boards to get you thinking. I'm going to give you a checklist of essentials for each inspiration board too. This checklist will become your new ingredient list of closet staples. It will make identifying what's missing from your wardrobe easy and will remind you not to go off-track at sales or get caught up in trendy items that don't fit your style. Make copies for your everyday bag and refrigerator, and keep one next to your computer for online shopping. Note that some items already in your closet will turn up on your inspiration board, and I've highlighted the most common ones for your list. Good for you! You've got a head-start.

# The Weekend Girl

**CELEB ICONS:**

Jennifer Aniston

Jennifer Garner

Halle Berry

Katie Holmes

Cameron Diaz

**SHE WEARS:**

- Anoraks
- A simple, unstructured bag
- Aviator or metal-rimmed sunglasses
- Big hoops and bohemian dangly earrings
- Chambray, denim, gingham, and plaid shirts
- Cords/jeans, slim ankle-cropped pants, and pencils
- Flat boots, Western-look cropped boots, beige suede boots

- Polished dress flats
- Flats—ballet slippers, slippers, loafers
- Flip-flops
- Hoodies and hooded sweaters (even cashmere ones)
- Jean jackets and jean shorts
- Jersey and knit dresses
- Knit jackets—cropped, wrapped, and blazers
- Knit sheaths and shifts
- Knit slim skirts
- Knit, slim, ankle-cropped pants
- Leather and suede jackets
- Leather jeans
- Leggings
- Low or stacked heels

- Light drapey scarves
- Military-look/safari/trench jackets
- Non-white sneakers, non-workout sneakers
- Quilted vests and puffers
- Relaxed dresses—maxi, wrap, tank, shift, shirtdress
- Khakis and cargos
- Slouchy sweaters and relaxed cardigans
- Trench coats
- Tanks
- Tees
- Tunics
- Vintage-wash jeans and ankle-cropped dark jeans
- Vintage-look belts with turquoise cowboy buckles
- Wedges

Weekend Girl has a relaxed, downtown, beachy, chic bohemian, sporty California style even if she lives in Iowa or New Jersey.

# The Girly Girl

**STYLE ICONS:**

Kelly Ripa

Taylor Swift

Katy Perry

Zooey Deschanel

Michelle Obama

**SHE WEARS:**

- Ankle-cropped pants and slim jeans in colors or prints
- Anything with ruffles, tiers, ribbons, embroidery, or crochet
- Bags with extra decorative details like bows, tassels, ties, or embellishments like stones or embroidery
- Belts to contour coats, cardigans, dresses
- Bow blouses
- Cap-toe shoes and quilted chain-strap bags
- Cardigans, especially embellished or trimmed ones
- Colorful tailored coats
- Colorful, fitted stretch jeans in colors like pink, rose, mint, or floral prints
- Delicate fabrics like silk, lace, chiffon, velvet
- Dress/jacket combos
- Dresses day and night in fit-and-flare, A-line, sheaths, and peplum styles
- Feminine heels like T-straps, peep-toes, strappy sandals
- Jeweled sandals
- Jewelry with sparkle or glow, especially stones and pearls
- Lacy camisoles and slips
- Lady jackets in pretty tweeds and boucles
- Leather peplum top or jacket
- Leather ruffle-trimmed jacket
- Quilted shoulder bags
- Silk shirts and sleeveless tops
- Sleeveless blouses with tiers, lace, beads, draped necklines
- Straight pants in a drapey, soft fabric like viscose, silk
- Skirts that swing or move—A-line, pleated, bell, or trumpet
- Skirts embellished with lace, sequins, embroidery, scallop hems
- Sweet colors like pink, rose, pastels, dreamy blues and violets, yellow, apricot
- Tiny prints, especially florals and dots

Girly Girl always has a feminine look even if she spikes her dresses with booties and a leather jacket.

15

# The Sophisticated Girl

**STYLE ICONS:**

Anne Hathaway

Lucy Liu

Ellen DeGeneres

Kate Middleton

**SHE WEARS:**

- Big, bold, black or tortoise sunglasses
- Blazers and structured jackets
- Chic totes in leather
- Classic flat-knit sweaters like crews, turtles, V-necks, boat-necks, cardigans
- Leather pencil skirt or jeans
- Classic jewelry like pearls, gold or silver cuffs, bangles and hoops, studs
- Crisp solid and striped button-downs—fitted, wrapped, or contoured
- Dress and coat duos
- Driving loafers and flats (ballet, slipper flats)
- Elegant slingbacks and pumps with stacked, block, tapered, or kitten heels; tapered toes
- Embossed leather and snakeskin bags
- Embossed belts and shoes
- Oxford lace-ups
- Reefer coats, pea coats
- Riding boots and cropped ankle boots
- Slim tailored pants and straight pants
- Structured shoulder bags and satchels
- Suits—matched and unmatched skirt suits and pantsuits
- Tailored pencil and A-line skirts
- Tailored dresses
- Tweed, plaid, herringbone, paisley
- White shirts

The Sophisticated Girl has a classic but not stuffy style, loves tailoring, structure, blazers, and clean lines.

# The Sexy Girl

**STYLE ICONS:**

Rihanna

Beyoncé

Jennifer Lopez

Kim Kardashian

Christina Aguilera

Gwen Stefani

**SHE WEARS:**

- Bandage dresses
- Belted jackets and coats
- Black cotton, microfiber, patent, or leather trench
- Biker and moto jackets in leather
- Booties
- Chains, buckles, studs, zippers, and grommets
- Classic high-heel pumps
- Cold-shoulder, one-shoulder, off-shoulder tops
- Dramatic necklines like deep Vs, scoops, and halters
- Feathers, fringe, and fur
- Funky blazers in brocade, metallics, or prints
- Jeans that are leather or faux, wax-coated, or metallic
- Jewelry with hardware accents
- Knee-high or over-the-knee boots with major heels
- Knee-high, leg-clinging stretch suede and leather boots with heels
- Leather leggings
- Leather sleeveless sheath or shift
- Leather and suede tailored jackets and blazers
- Lots of leopard, cheetah, and python
- Metallic bags
- Minis
- Neons
- Oversized or statement sunglasses and glasses
- Pencil skirts tapered to fit
- Platform pumps and sandals
- Ruched jersey tops, skirts, and dresses
- Sheaths with curve-hugging fit
- Stilettos
- Sweaterdresses
- Wrap dresses
- Wrap tops and coats

Sexy Girl has attention-getting style but knows how far to go. She shows her shape and never misses a chance for some leather, shimmer, and bling.

# THE OMG! MOMENT

UH-OH...JUST LOOKED AT YOUR CLOSET AND IT FEELS EMPTY? DON'T PANIC. LESS IS MORE, AND THAT'S NOT A CLICHÉ WHEN YOU'RE WARDROBE BUILDING. STAY COMMITTED TO YOUR STYLE NOW THAT YOU KNOW WHAT THAT STYLE IS! CREATING YOUR ULTIMATE SUCCESSFUL WARDROBE IS NOT GOING TO HAPPEN IN A DAY. IT TAKES TIME AND DISCIPLINE. THINK ABOUT ALL THE SPUR-OF-THE-MINUTE PURCHASES YOU'VE MADE THAT ENDED UP BEING BAD BUYS.

By editing out the losers, you are doing exactly what top stylists do for their clients. You'd be surprised how many times packed closets and racks of clothes get weeded down to a handful of "successful" items. Honestly, the more "wrong" clothes left in your closet, the harder it will be to put together successful looks, and this is your new goal every single day.

You need to establish a consistent look. What separates a style icon from the pack (and from other celebs) is that icons are super consistent in what they select to wear. Photo after photo, they own their look. Even celebrities make mistakes when they go outside their best look. Some spend endless amounts of money on clothes that don't work for their bodies or get talked into trends that don't suit them by stylists who are more interested in getting their designer chum's clothes on famous folks in the news. These celebs end up on worst-dressed lists or get panned in magazines and wonder why?!

You need to de-friend your closet and detach from clothes that won't help you achieve your inspiration board look. Go through the racks, shelves, and boxes and pull out whatever isn't on your inspiration board checklist. It's important to get these things out of your closet and out of the way before you start having regrets. Gazing at a bunch of rejects in big, overstuffed plastic bags is too tempting. You don't want to feel bad about the purple plaid dress you bought on sale and never wore, or the asymmetric skirt that felt like a Halloween costume, or those red jeans that looked great online but not on you. Lose the guilt and turn this purge into a positive moneymaking solution by selling it all on eBay or at a consignment shop, flea market, or tag sale.

While you're at it, also pull out any item that is too small, too tight, or too uncomfortable to wear. If your weight or body has changed, don't apologize to your clothes or wait for the day when your old body reappears. Be realistic too about clothes that look tacky and tired. This is a good time to get rid of pilled sweaters, leggings and tights that have lost their cling, the jeans that don't come close to zipping (and haven't for years), anything stained or sloppy (like your old college sweatshirts and boyfriend sweaters), trippy neon tanks, and big boxy jackets that do nothing for you. Let it go!

# SUCCESS FOR LESS

Let's have the money talk. I know you're wondering how to achieve your style goals without cashing in your 401K or racking up more credit card bills you can't afford. Slow and steady is our plan. There are three tricks to spending less and looking better that I promise are painless. I'm going to share them with you: Swap, Sell, Save! And yes, there will be some shopping to do to get your look in shape no matter how resourceful you are. Just don't plan on doing it all in one day.

### Swap it.

Get together with your girlfriends at your place and trade all the style-wrecking clothes and accessories that were clogging your closet. What's not right for you will work for someone else. Throw in some cocktails and snacks and you have a fun evening and a no-sweat, stress-free way to get rid of the excess. There's no packing up or hauling stuff away. Just provide a box of clean, fresh trash bags for your chums. Swapping is a style-sharing solution that benefits all. No money is needed, and you get to upgrade your closet and fill that checklist.

### Sell it.

It's your choice where, but eBay, consignment shops, tag sales, flea markets, and Craigslist all offer opportunities. Your rejects can generate new dollars to invest back into your successful style plan. There's an endless community of entrepreneurs selling and bartering clothes and accessories at market value. You do need to make the effort to photograph and catalog items for online sales and stay on top of items being sold for you by others if you go the consignment route, but it's worth it.

### Save it.

One of my favorite things to do is repurpose a "wrong" garment and make it right for my look. If an item of clothing or accessory has great quality, a good cut, and attractive details, you can give it a new identity. Dresses can become tunics or tops to wear with jeans; jackets can be tapered, shortened, or transformed into vests; hip belts can become waist belts. You can even dye distressed or bleached-out jeans dark. Think like a stylist. When I'm faced with a rack of clothes and a client that are a clear mismatch, being able to rework items is crucial. Sewing skills, by the way, are back and not just for budding designers. Wouldn't it be great to be able to tweak your own clothes and do hems without paying tailoring bills?

# GRETTA'S STYLE-FOR-LESS STAKEOUT

I know you're anxious to buy just one new thing to move the success needle in your direction. Starting with an inexpensive item or two will give you confidence in your new power to determine what works for you. Whether you're shopping at the mall, online, or by mail, keep these five tips in mind.

## Look for fabrics or close-enough fakes.

Fashion magazines can be inspirational but misleading. No one is really going to spend $20,000 on a crocodile bag or $3,000 on a dress for work—not when you've got a mortgage, student loans, kids, and basic monthly bills to pay! There are plenty of synthetic fabrics that mimic expensive ones. Blends with a touch of the real thing (like cashmere or silk) provide a similar look and feel. If you're aiming for the real thing, sales and online flash sales offer the chance to upgrade items for your look with authentic luxury fabrics. Add pieces in faux or real leather, suede, and silk. Add cashmere, snakeskin, and fur or fur trim to any of the four categories to bring texture to your clothes. It's the mix of textures that makes an outfit successful, whether you're wearing a faux-fur vest with jeans or a silk chiffon blouse and leather skirt. Embossed leathers like mock croc, faux python, and ostrich are great, and so are faux-fur belts and bags stenciled to resemble cheetah, leopard, or zebra. Even low-cost jersey dresses and silk polyester blouses have a more luxurious look in an animal print. One of my favorite stores when it comes to low-cost quality-look fabrics is Zara—everything appears ten times more expensive than the actual cost. You need to read the tag twice to believe it!

## Shop inexpensive items as if they're super luxurious.

Hunt through low-cost stores for bargains exactly as you would at the most expensive exclusive stores. Be picky about the merchandise too. Just because an item is $20 instead of $200 doesn't mean you should ring it up. You need to be selective about inexpensive clothes and accessories to be a successful wardrobe worker. Be prepared to reject items that look poorly made or badly finished, are too exaggerated in shape, or have cheesy details that can't be changed. (FYI, things like buttons and self-belts can be changed.)

*Nothing is worse than lookalike accessories, especially bags with imitation logos.*

### Stay away from knockoffs.

Nothing is worse than look-alike accessories, especially bags with imitation logos. When low-cost manufacturers imitate higher-priced signature brands with nearly identical hardware and patterns, they're not helping you look successful. The real bag picked up at a vintage store is a better option if you're dead-set on a particular brand. What's even better is to look for a quality-look bag that's not trying to fool anyone.

### Shop fast fashion for costume jewelry, but keep it simple.

Basics like gold hoops, cubic zirconia studs, bangles, stackable rings, simple cuffs, and statement pearls are easy to find at a mass-market level. They look real enough to fool a pro. For intricate pieces with a one-of-a-kind antique look, I like to seek the real thing for less at (you guessed it!) secondhand stores, where the good stuff turns up surprisingly often.

### Cheap replicas of trendier fashion do work.

Stay away from extremes, and do your homework. Use magazines or comparison-shop online to get the price point you can afford and the look you want. Turn down anything that looks obviously cheap, like an overdose of sparkle, too many sequins, or any fabric that looks flammable!

# SO WHAT'S YOU?

You now know exactly whether your "look" is essentially Weekend, Girly, Sophisticated, or Sexy. You also have your checklist of the "ingredients" you need to make your look work. But just knowing which look is the one you want to achieve is not enough to go on at this point. Hang on to your inspiration board and keep updating it as new photos and clips within your look grab your attention. The board will remind you to stay on track. Keep those starter items simmering too because they provide a reliable base for new-look pieces—those flavors and spices—you'll be adding to your fashion stock. Your best personal wardrobe recipes will evolve over the following chapters. You will learn the important details about each item on your checklist so you avoid shopping mistakes. You'll learn which of your ingredients mix, blend, or layer well together and why. And you'll find out how to really put the pieces together successfully every time, no matter what body, age, or financial issues are on your mind.

## What's wrong with this picture?

Right now, you're probably wondering if my inspiration board method is goof-proof. The answer is yes unless you fall into one of two personalities: the girl who knows too much or the girl who knows too little. The girl who knows too much is way too rigid, has ironclad rules about clothes, and is stuck in a time warp when it comes to selecting the right proportions. She can't let go enough to try something new, even if it means finally getting closer to the style that she wants. The girl who knows too little is afraid of fashion. She always looks unfinished and unpolished and appears timid about making a style statement even if it may get her life to the next level of success and happiness. Let me show you one example of what we're talking about. These three girls have selected the "girly" inspiration board and an LBD, but only one is on the road to successful style.

### THE GIRL WHO KNOWS TOO MUCH
is wearing her LBD too short, too tight, too extreme. She's added fussy, busy, overloaded shoes, too much jewelry, makeup, and over-styled hair.

### THE GIRL WHO KNOWS TOO LITTLE
is wearing her LBD too long, loose and frumpy. She's bare-faced, has unpolished unstyled hair and makes no effort. She's got on frumpy worn-out flats and no jewelry.

### THE SUCCESSFUL GIRL is wearing her LBD at the right above-the-knees length, with her booties, a stack of bracelets, contemporary makeup and freshly styled hair.

# THE GRETTA STYLE-OVER

after

Stephanie headed straight for the Sexy Girl inspiration board. She loves her curves, but when I met her she was dressing in boxy black basics that hid them. I showed her how fitted dresses enhance her silhouette day or night and how wearing pale neutrals or subtle shimmer flatters her skin tone. Asymmetric necklines, knee-length hemlines, and heels are her new go-tos.

before

# CHAPTER 2

# THE 24/7 STYLE DIET

THE SUCCESSFUL GIRL doesn't let time depriva-
tion or a crazy nonstop schedule affect her style.
How do I know? Because, like you, I live a 24/7
multitasking lifestyle. My no-fail system can keep
us both dressed right and ready for anything
Monday to Sunday.

We all juggle some combo of work, kids, family, and social life. Take that daily to-do list and
add all the unexpected extras that weren't there
a minute ago—the visit to the dentist, the vet,
parent/teacher conference, your lawyer, your real
estate broker, a last-minute
client dinner—and you have a
stressful time crunch. Getting
dressed with style and speed is
the last thing we want to think
about. And yet, we do because
the cold, hard truth is that we
need to look good all day for
every situation. In the best
possible scenario, we'd like to
accomplish that without changing our clothes. Whether we're
stay-at-home moms, teachers,
pharmacists, research analysts, executive assistants,
computer programmers, or work part-time in sales,
we all have one thing in common: Our days never
follow a neat little plan. Well, guess what? Your
clothes certainly can! The secret lies in your inspiration board and its checklist of essentials.

Like foodies who manage their weight with a
strict regimen but still find calorie-free ways to
indulge their cravings, a 24/7 style diet helps
fashion-loving girls tackle multitasking days while
sticking to their look in a satisfying way. It starts
with a simple clothes recipe that's lean, mean, and
hardworking but spicy enough so you don't get
bored. It'll help trim the fat from your closet and
help you ultimately edit out items (even some you
may have craved) that aren't truly working for
your life. Best of all, it will get you through long
days with confidence and flair.

The 24/7 style diet is simple. It follows a few
preplanned outfits or "uniforms" (in fashion
lingo) that provide a formula. All you do is put
the appropriate pieces together. Take a look at

> *Use my simple clothes recipe to get you through the days with confidence and flair.*

your inspiration board checklist and the board
itself to learn which pieces work together consistently again and again. These pieces will provide
the core of your 24/7 wardrobe and take the daily
what-to-wear-today issue off the table. Every
morning all you need to do is change up the items,
relying on color, style, texture, and fit for variety.

My uniform system has my Gretta guarantee:
It's so easy and foolproof, you won't be tempted
to "cheat" or fall off the style wagon. It'll also
help you establish a consistent, recognizable style.

# THE GOTTA-HAVES

**This is your multitasking kit for success**

24/7 MEANS TWENTY-FOUR HOURS A DAY, SEVEN DAYS A WEEK, 365 DAYS A YEAR. IN STYLE TERMS, THAT TRANSLATES TO A DEPENDABLE CORE WARDROBE OF EVERYDAY CLOTHES AND ACCESSORIES THAT YOU CAN QUICKLY PULL TOGETHER AND KNOW THAT THEY WILL WORK ANYWHERE, ANYTIME. WITH JUST MINOR TWEAKS FROM YOU, YOUR UNIFORM DRESSES UP OR DRESSES DOWN. THERE ARE DAYS YOU WILL WANT TO GET DRESSED FIRST THING IN THE MORNING AND KEEP THAT OUTFIT GOING WAY INTO THE NIGHT, NOT JUST NINE TO FIVE. TEN GOTTA-HAVE 24/7 ITEMS WORK FOR EACH OF THE FOUR STYLE GROUPS. THEY WILL GET YOU HEADED IN THE RIGHT DIRECTION.

THEY WILL SAVE YOU ON DAYS WHEN YOU'RE SLAMMED AND WONDERING HOW YOU CAN DO IT ALL. A MULTITASKING WARDROBE STRATEGY CAN GET YOU THROUGH EXHAUSTING DAYS OF FAMILY EVENTS, WORK SITUATIONS, AND EVERY WHAT-DO-I-WEAR-NOW CRISIS. THEY GIVE YOU THE SPIRIT TO JUMP THE LINE, SNAG THE PARKING SPOT, ANSWER THE AD, GO TO THE INTERVIEW, AND GET OFF THE COUCH TO MEET FRIENDS FOR COCKTAILS OR BRUNCH.

START FROM THE BOTTOM UP AND BUILD A BASE FOR LAYERS AND EXTRAS.

## 1. SHOES YOU CAN RUN, DRIVE, OR DANCE IN

No matter what your style, every girl needs speedy footwear. The choice of flats, low heels, wedges, chunky platform heels, or sneakers is yours. Remember, you can always stash a pair of higher, slimmer heels in your bag, car, or under your desk and slip into them for meetings, dates, or dinner, or fold-up ballet flats (now even found in drugstore racks) in your bag.

**BEST CHOICE** A metallic flat that styles up anything.

## 4. A SKINNY BOTTOM PIECE TO ANCHOR YOUR OUTFIT

Start with a slim base like fitted jeans, ankle-cropped pants, leggings, a pencil skirt, or a dress that's straight and trim from the waist down (anything from a sheath to a shift or a sweaterdress). Keeping the lower half of your silhouette narrow gives you more flexibility, speed, and flattery in selecting top pieces. You can add layers, a soft full blouse, any jacket, or a slouchy sweater and know it works.

**BEST CHOICE** Choose black or any dark color for slim-ability and mixability. (See chapter 6 for more figure flattery.) Make these skinny basics wardrobe staples, and buy duplicates of these items when you see them on sale.

## 2. THIN KNITS

Light tanks, tees, bodysuits, and very fine-gauge knit pullovers layer easily and keep you comfortable in any climate. They don't add bulk to your shape and enable you to bare your body or cover up as needed.

**BEST CHOICE** Bodysuits or tanks and tees toned to your bottom piece or one another work together as stylish layers. Simply peel off or add on as your day progresses. A tank or tee studded with stones or sequins can go glam solo, or just add a statement necklace or an embellished cardigan and you're ready to party.

## 3. PRINTS

Patterns are 24/7 regulars because they don't show stains, creases, bulges, or jiggles. They're ideal choices that take the worry out of kid-centric activities, travel, and meals on the run (less worry about spills and drips!).

**BEST CHOICE** Small- to medium-scale prints in an overall pattern spice up a one-color look and are complimentary to all figure types. (See page 44 for more print-combining strategies.)

## 5. CARDIGANS

This one item is now a huge clothes category on its own. It includes zip-ups, hoodies, wraps, classic V and jewel-neck cardigans, long boyfriend cardigans, and cardigans embellished with stones, sequins, fringe, and fur. They provide a quick throw-on layer that gives you leverage over the weather and air conditioning and adds extra style. Cropped waist-length cardigans provide instant arm coverage for sleeveless dresses and bare tops but still show your shape. They also work over A-line dresses or skirts when you want to emphasize waist definition. Longer thigh-length cardigans provide instant camouflage for hips and booty when wearing jeans and slim pants.

**BEST CHOICE** A v-neck body-skimming hip-length cardigan in a flat knit.

## 6. WARDROBE PIECES IN THE SAME COLOR GROUP

Plan your style wardrobe in one or two favorite colors, but vary the shades from light to dark to medium. This lets you mix and layer and combine solids with prints, or even prints with prints, you know definitely work together. It gets you dressed fast without fuss.

**BEST CHOICE** A favorite color worn head-to-toe in varying shades and textures is a 24/7 mood booster (See pages 40–41 for further color-mixing ideas).

## 7. WRAP DRESSES

Available in comfy, fluid fabrics from affordable jersey and ponte knits to pricey cashmere, wrap dresses provide a one-stop base for super-rushed days. They give every girl instant body-friendly shaping by defining or creating a waist, while the V neckline elongates your neck and trims your torso.

**BEST CHOICE** A real, honest-to-goodness adjustable wrap with a tie that you can control so the dress molds to your exact curves. Forget faux-wraps—they don't provide the same benefits at all.

## 8. A TRENCH COAT

The ultimate multifunctional, all-season coat to depend on day or night, rain or shine. Look for classic water-resistant fabrics blends and traditional details like the belt (which you knot, not buckle!) and epaulettes.

**BEST CHOICE** A beige, classic, go-everywhere iconic trench that's about knee length.

## 9. SUNGLASSES

Big, fashionable sunglasses offer speedy camouflage till you get your eye makeup on or serve as eye candy on no-makeup days. They buy time when your eyes are puffy, tired, red, or teary too.

**BEST CHOICE** Your best shape and size in a sexy classic like metal-rimmed aviators or big, bold, oversized black or tortoise frames. Choose dark gray or green UV-protected lenses for driving and pale, tinted, cosmetic lenses when you need to make eye contact.

## 10. A CARRY-ALL BAG

Your ideal bag is roomy but light, with outside zippered compartments and inside pockets or compartments to securely stow your electronics and valuables. It should be big enough to carry a clutch inside for days when you have events or after-work dates. You then can check the big bag and just carry your essentials.

**BEST CHOICE** Choose a color that works with your wardrobe theme and can handle 24/7 versatility. It can blend in or provide a dash of color to a dark or neutral wardrobe. Keep in mind that embossed, pebble-grained, and textured bags in snakeskin, faux ostrich, and croc don't show as much wear as smooth leathers. Deep, rich, dark colors show dirt less than light ones. If your bag has a black or dark lining, stick to bright or print accessories for your wallet, iPhone case, and makeup kit.

# THE 24/7 FORMULA FOR STYLE

NOW WHAT? YOU'VE GOT YOUR STARTER KIT (AND FEEL FREE TO ADD IN SOME OF THOSE PIECES THAT WORK FOR YOUR NEW LOOK TOO). YOU'VE CREATED AN INSPIRATION BOARD AND FOUND YOUR REAL STYLE ALONG WITH A CHECKLIST OF CLOTHES AND ACCESSORIES TO GET YOUR NEW LOOK OFF THE GROUND.

The next step is to take a closer look at the board and checklist and select the pieces to build your basic core look. You may even have two or three core looks within your style. They work as a 24/7 foundation or "uniform" you can depend on every day of the year. This "uniform" provides a no-fail system for pulling together your look quickly and with a minimum of time, thought, and decision-making. It's preplanned, like a frozen entrée, and all you need to do is heat it up with the right accessories. Once you get the basic look down, getting creative with color, texture, and prints makes the 24/7 uniform irresistible.

Let's say, for example, that you're a girly girl, and your 24/7 "uniform" is a dress, cardigan, and stacked-heel pumps. You'd wear different versions of that dress, cardigan, and pumps look but keep the recipe the same. You're staying within your style but "seasoning" it by changing color, texture, and details. Maybe one day you'd be in a pink A-line dress, rosy-red beaded cardigan, and nude stacked heels, and the next in a floral dress, pink cardigan, and patent T-straps. It's a can't-miss recipe for success when you shop and dress. Here are some core strategies or "uniforms" for the four girl looks we discussed in chapter 1. Use them as a starting point, and feel free to make changes as you master the concept.

## Gretta-quette

We are all 24/7 Successful Girls each with our own life and style. For me this was one of those days. It started at 5:30 a.m. and ended at 11 p.m. with only a quick stop home to feed, read, and put my son, Kai, to bed before going to judge the DailyGlow Beauty Innovator Awards (an honor since I love this site!). This silk blouse and leather skirt look works for long on-the-go days. The dark leather skirt camouflages spills and smudges and is wrinkle free, while the silk print blouse is eye-catching and feminine—that mix of soft and tough makes it modern. All this quick "uniform" needed was dark tights and booties for a fast finish.

*or*                    *or*

Leggings
+ layered tanks and tees
+ ballet flats or boots
+ a soft, unstructured jacket
+ a drapey scarf

**TO DRESS IT DOWN** Remove the jacket or swap it for a cardigan or jean jacket.

**TO DRESS IT UP** Add big hoops or dangly earrings, and a scarf or flats with sparkle, or swap your plain top for a metallic or sequin one.

Cargos or cords + a tank
+ a slouchy sweater
+ wedges or sneakers
+ a jean, military look, or soft leather jacket

**TO DRESS IT DOWN** Opt for sneakers or flip-flops, and wear a plaid shirt or the jean jacket as a top layer.

**TO DRESS IT UP** Go for the wedge or do a strappy sandal, take off the sweater, and wear the leather jacket solo; add your statement pendant necklace.

A relaxed dress
+ a slouchy cardigan
+ boots, ballet flats, or booties
+ a soft leather jacket

**TO DRESS IT DOWN** Trade the leather jacket for a jean jacket, and do flats.

**TO DRESS IT UP** Take off the cardigan, wear booties and the leather jacket with the dress, and add your hoops or dangly earrings.

# IF YOU'RE A **Girly Girl**
## YOUR 24/7 UNIFORM MIGHT BE

*or*     *or*

**A sleeveless dress**
+ **a lady jacket or tailored coat**
+ **platforms or booties**
+ **pearls**

**TO DRESS IT DOWN** Add a trench or leather jacket instead of the lady jacket or tailored coat; opt for dress flats or low heels.

**TO DRESS IT UP** Swap platforms or booties for jeweled sandals and a clutch, take off the jacket and coat, add a statement necklace or an armful of bracelets, and belt the dress for shape.

**A bow blouse**
+ **a skirt**
+ **a cardigan**
+ **T-straps or Mary Janes**

**TO DRESS IT DOWN** Do booties and swap the bow blouse for a fitted sweater.

**TO DRESS IT UP** Go for a higher heel in a peep-toe or strappy sandal, and take off the cardigan or swap it for an embellished one; add more sparkle with earrings and a glam bag.

**Colorful jeans or slim ankle-cropped pants**
+ **a silk top**
+ **a cardigan or jacket**
+ **sparkly jeweled sandals or cap-toe flats**

**TO DRESS IT DOWN** Go for the jeans, cardigan, and flat sandals.

**TO DRESS IT UP** Do the cropped pants or jeans with a jacket, a higher-heel pump or decorative high heel sandal, and add your statement necklace or bracelets and a clutch.

# IF YOU'RE A **Sophisticated Girl**
## YOUR 24/7 UNIFORM MIGHT BE

*or*          *or*

A belted tailored sheath
+ **matching coat**
+ **slingbacks or pumps**

**TO DRESS IT DOWN** Take off the belt, do low pumps or booties, and add a cardigan or leather jacket instead of the coat.

**TO DRESS IT UP** Opt for higher heels in an unexpected color or metallic, and add a statement necklace and a decorative bag with stones or bow details.

A skirt suit or pantsuit
+ **a flat-knit sweater or sleeveless top**
+ **boots or pumps**

**TO DRESS IT DOWN** Remove the jacket or swap jeans for the bottom piece.

**TO DRESS IT UP** Swap a silk blouse for the sweater, pile on your classic jewelry (cuffs or bangles, studs or hoops), and do higher-heel pumps.

A crisp white shirt
+ **slim ankle cropped pants**
+ **a blazer**
+ **loafers or flats**

**TO DRESS IT DOWN** Do the white shirt with jeans and loafers, and add a pea coat or cardigan instead of the blazer.

**TO DRESS IT UP** Trade the loafers or flats for slingbacks or pumps, and add an embossed leather bag and belt. Do a structured blazer in a dressier fabric like a cashmere/wool blend or velvet or brocade for an even dressier look.

# IF YOU'RE A **Sexy Girl**
## YOUR 24/7 UNIFORM MIGHT BE

*or*    *or*

Leggings
+ a mini
+ over-the knee boots
+ a sweater
+ a faux fur or leather jacket

**TO DRESS IT DOWN** Do leggings and boots without the mini.

**TO DRESS IT UP** Swap the sweater for a body-hugging wrapped, ruched, or draped top, and trade the leggings for tights in a color or pattern.

Skinny jeans + a tank
+ a low-neck sweater
+ a leather jacket or funky blazer
+ biker boots or stilettos

**TO DRESS IT DOWN** Do the biker boots and leather jacket, skip the blazer, and consider swapping in a fitted tee or sweater with a higher neck for the low.

**TO DRESS IT UP** Go for the stilettos and a more fitted sweater or a halter top, and load up on your hardware jewelry.

A jersey dress + tights
+ a funky blazer
+ black patent or leather trench
+ hardware-adorned booties

**TO DRESS IT DOWN** Do the dress but lose the blazer, and do a flat biker boot.

**TO DRESS IT UP** Skip the blazer and do a lacy tight, or go bare-legged, swap the booties for a high studded pump, and add lots of chain-link jewelry and a standout bag in a metallic or animal print.

# GRETTA'S STRATEGY WHEEL

WE ALL LIVE DIFFERENT LIVES EVEN WHEN WE HAVE SIMILAR LIFESTYLES, AGES, OR JOBS. THE AMOUNT OF TIME WE SPEND ON WORK, PARENTING, SOCIALIZING, EXERCISE, ERRANDS, AND DOWNTIME VARIES FROM GIRL TO GIRL. IT ALL AFFECTS THE KINDS OF CLOTHES WE BUY AND EMPHASIZE IN OUR WARDROBE.

You might be a twenty-two-year-old college grad temping part-time while interviewing for a real full-time job and dating on nights and weekends. You might be a married stay-at-home mom with two-plus kids who is always on the go, chasing a toddler, running errands, taking your baby to play-group, and keeping the family lifestyle going full-speed with as few speed bumps as possible. Or you might be a single working mom with one child in kindergarten and one in day care whose main concerns right now are work and parenting.

Our clothes priorities and needs continue to change as our lives evolve, even though our style may stay pretty much the same. For example, a divorced mom who works nine to five and dates will have a different balance of clothes in her wardrobe than a married-no-kids girl who is climbing the corporate ladder and traveling for work, even if they are both "girly girls." A stay-at-home mom who is CEO of her household and does not work will have a different balance of clothes in her closet than a mom in real estate sales with two dogs, a live-in boyfriend, and two kids in elementary school, even if they are both stylish "sophisticated girls."

Every girl's life includes six possible components: work, parenting, socializing, exercise, errands, and downtime. Within those six, the time and importance you devote to each depends on your individual life and needs.

## Here's how it plays out:

**WORK** How and where you work and what you do influences your 24/7 style choices. You might work from home (but attend Skype meetings where the dress code is businesslike) or spend weekdays in an office cubicle where your job is accomplished almost entirely over the phone or at the computer. You may sit all day, or stand all day, or be dashing from one meeting to another. Maybe you work face-to-face with a revolving door of customers or clients. Perhaps your job involves lots of commuting or walking. Maybe you work outdoors or spend time outdoors as part of your job. If you work part-time or full-time, multiple jobs or evenings only, that plays into your strategy too.

**PARENTING** Where does your parenting role fit in to you 24/7 style? You may be a full-time stay-at-home mom or a working mom who spends time with the kids after work and on weekends. Maybe you're divorced or separated and have every other weekend free or have stepkids to parent only on weekends. Maybe your parenting involves playdates or coaching sports, frequent carpooling, or lots of hands-on time at home, supervising projects and going over homework. Maybe you're pregnant or adopting a child now, and your style needs are due to change.

**SOCIALIZING** How much time do your spend seeing friends, family, and others? You may be dating or in a relationship and frequently go out for dinner, coffee, or drinks during the week and on weekends. Maybe you're single, networking, and looking for a partner 24/7. Maybe you're a big-family girl and have the folks, neighbors, and/or your extended family and friends over on weekends or go to their houses. If you're in entertainment, PR, or a corporate workplace, chances are you have business lunches or dinners with clients or business-related events to attend. Now that e-mail invites are the rule, who knows what drop-by events you might have added to your agenda?

**EXERCISE** Does fitness fit into your 24/7 schedule? Maybe your idea of exercise is walking the dog before and after work or doing sit-ups while watching morning news on TV. Maybe you're an at-home yoga-DVD girl, or a three-times-a-week gym bunny, or maybe you take fitness seriously and are training for a marathon. Maybe you swim at the Y year-round or you're a Saturdays-and-Sundays-only weekend warrior. Maybe biking or Rollerblading with your kids is your only fitness routine.

**ERRANDS** Who doesn't have tasks like getting gas, grocery shopping, and dashing to the drugstore and dry cleaner on their daily to-do list? What about getting a haircut, bringing clothes to the tailor, picking up pet food or takeout, buying birthday presents, or shopping for new jeans, a bra, or glasses? These extras are endless whether planned or spur-of-the-minute. And who wants to run into their boss or ex in old sweats?

**DOWNTIME** You need alone time too—time to recharge and veg out. Maybe you read or play the piano, take a cooking class on Wednesday evenings, or just listen to your iPod as you straighten up the house. Maybe you take "me" time at work by window-shopping online or by using your lunch hour or commuting time to catch up on call-backs and e-mails or read. Maybe your mini "downtime" is a leisurely coffee at a neighborhood shop on the way to work or between meetings.

---

**Here's an example of how the 24/7 wardrobe is a total success and where it flops.**

**THE GIRL WHO KNOWS TOO MUCH** overdoes her be-prepared-for-anything attitude by piling on too many items that don't work together or give her a consistent look. She may wear trendy red jeans that are too tight and too low-rise with knee-high, high-heel stiletto boots (not exactly dressed for speed or versatility or a long day at work or home) and a trendy lace tee under a long, chunky, asymmetric sweater, all under a heavy puffer, while also carrying two bags (a big heavy hobo with no compartments in a nonversatile pastel and an old tote filled to overflowing with extras and a change of shoes, jewelry, and bra).

**THE GIRL WHO KNOWS TOO LITTLE** is never ready for anything, always under-dressed and apologizing for it. She is wearing red baggy "boyfriend" jeans, Uggs, and a plain white tee under a long, chunky, Fair Isle cabled boyfriend sweater and carrying a backpack stuffed with everything she might need.

**THE SUCCESSFUL GIRL** gets it right! She is wearing red slim ankle-cropped pants, a rosy-pink print blouse, a shocking pink cardigan, and nude low heels, and is carrying a big, slim bag in camel with zippered compartments.

# THE OMG! MOMENT

It would be great if all life boiled down to was work and play, but life gets messy, and we all have so much more to do in the same amount of time. The schedule and plan today is different for every woman. Analysts and financial planners use diagrams in the shape of wheels or pies to break down a project or business plan into manageable slices. They help visualize how time and money will be best spent. I apply this same theory to style and success, and you can too.

For simplicity's sake, here are four of the most common style strategy wheels. Take a look and see which comes closest to your own life. You may realize, "OMG! I didn't realize how much time I spend socializing, and my wardrobe doesn't reflect that," or "I need more work clothes, not more dating clothes, right now." Then apply this knowledge to your own 24/7 wardrobe planning.

*Works from home or part-time*

*Stay-at-home mom*

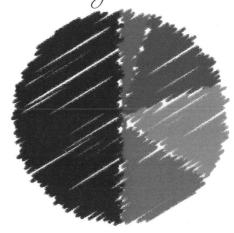

*Single mom who works and dates*

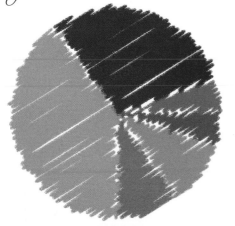

*Working career woman 9 to 5*

# AND KEEP IN MIND...

As I said earlier, your core uniforms give you an everyday basic recipe for dressing that lasts from dawn to dusk and keeps your look recognizable and steady. All you need to do is swap in pieces to vary color, texture, print, and accessories. This preplanned system saves you time in the a.m. and provides enough wiggle room for extras depending on your day and situation.

This is exactly how iconic women operate their closets and stay within their looks. You'll be adjusting these core looks as your life changes and your ability to manipulate clothes gains conviction. The most successful core looks last despite trends because you aren't making the mistake of jumping on every new fad. The one thing you do need to know is how to fine-tune each core look for your dress up/dress down needs of the day.

Most of us have fairly predictable daily schedules, even if they include several very different venues. The success of your core uniform depends on your ability to layer and accessorize. An extra layering piece or two gives you total control of your comfort despite what the weather, air-conditioning, or thermostat say. It also helps you choose what to camouflage, what to display, and when. Accessories keep your uniform fluid and help it transform from day to evening, casual to all business, serious to sexy, so you never feel overdressed or underdressed.

None of the old fashion rules apply anymore. Now that 24/7 multitasking lifestyles are the new normal, we wear leather and suede in summer, go sleeveless in winter, choose pastels in January and boots in July, and throw on sequins for work and leggings for evenings out. We expect maximum wear and flexibility all year, no matter what our personal style. The boundaries that used to define what was acceptable for certain seasons, times of day or night, occasions, and even our jobs are out the window. As a stylist, I know that 24/7 dressing is a great way to make maximum use of color, prints, and fabric texture because that's where your personality comes through. Here's how to make them work for you.

*Be a success despite stress + mess.*

# COLOR

Color instant-messages your mood. Choice of color(s) is one of the most personal decisions you make about clothes and can affect how you look and feel throughout a busy day. Check your inspiration board to see which colors pop up again and again. These are clearly your favorites, even if you don't currently own any items in those hues. Maybe you've always loved blues but stuck to black for security or camouflage. If so, it's time to start swapping black for dark, moody blues like navy, indigo, sapphire, and lapis and adding hits of baby and powder blue, turquoise, cobalt, and periwinkle for a 24/7 mix that will make you smile every morning.

Remember, your inspiration boards are a guide, but you do have room to experiment once you get your core looks together. Having the right pieces and knowing how to put it all together for a consistent look come first. Color "loves" count, but you still need to stick to a color theme. This is

## All sorbet, powdery, and pastel colors work together.

Baby blue, mint, butter, pale pink, dove gray, vanilla, lavender, apricot, peach, aquamarine, rose, and celadon are totally compatible blended together.

**TIP:** These muted tints look romantic and feminine when paired or layered tone on tone. Add nude shoes for a subtle, seamless look or sharpen the sweet look with black accessories.

## All rich, warm, natural colors work together.

Forest greens like fern, pine, and olive; earthy browns like sienna, chestnut, terra-cotta, cinnamon, and tan; and the rusty reds and oranges of autumn leaves like amber, golden yellow, carnelian, auburn, and russet are easy to blend in the same outfit.

**TIP:** These colors rock when layered—even a peek of a color in a tank, sleeve, collar, or bow makes the look. Think of how sunsets and landscapes melt colors into one another for ideas. For example, just the collar and soft tie of a golden yellow bow blouse under a cropped brown leather jacket provide a hint of color.

the best way to simplify your routine and make the most of your wardrobe whether you have 20 pieces or 200! You may eventually end up being a girly girl who likes non-colors like white and charcoal, or a sophisticated girl who prefers soft pastels. It doesn't change your style; it takes it one step further and personalizes it.

As a stylist, I also encourage women to mix colors in new ways to energize a wardrobe. When you wear the same kinds of pieces frequently (and when you have successful style, you do!), playing around with color gives you plenty of room for variation, so you're never bored or tempted to stray from your formula. Color gives your wardrobe dimension. Here are some color mixes I find always work well together for multitasking lifestyles and can be adapted to whichever of the four "girls" you happen to be.

## All brights, primary colors, and jewel tones work together.

The brights, like fuchsia, brilliant pink, daffodil yellow, violet, cobalt, chartreuse, orange, and lipstick red, are all closet friends. Emerald, sapphire, topaz, ruby, and amethyst are too, and the three primary crayon colors, yellow, blue, and red, can always be boldly combined.

**TIP:** Pick one of the three groups and work for high contrast. For example, you might wear a bright pink dress with a lipstick red coat or cardigan, or your dark blue ankle-cropped jeans with a slouchy sapphire blue sweater and an emerald scarf, or olive cargos with a rusty tee and pine green cardigan.

## All non-colors work together.

Black, navy, charcoal, and white make perfect mates, and you can't possibly go wrong.

**TIP:** Each of these can also work tone on tone with similar colors. For example, charcoal can look great with its cool sister colors smoke, silver, slate blue, and greige, while white can look amazing with cream, eggshell, almond, and bisque colors.

Choice of color is one of the most personal decisions you make about clothes.

# FABRIC

I keep saying rules are over, and that means for texture too—any fabric goes! We wear sequins, satin, and see-through fabrics during the day now and combine lace with leather or suede with chiffon. In fact, fabrics that used to be mostly limited to the bridal market like organza, taffeta, satin, tulle, lace, and brocade are now used in streetwear and in everyday, ordinary clothes like jeans and tees. I am an admitted texture freak and will always prefer something with a little extra sizzle in the material to a flat matte finish. I love embossed leathers, a pearl embellished collar on a blouse, a splash of sequins on a sweater, a hint of crotchet in a skirt, insets or overlays of tulle, and lace or

### No fabric is taboo.

Environmental changes have made the one-season wardrobe a reality. We have learned to layer clothes, and designers have tweaked certain fabrics to make them more cross-seasonal. For example, leather, suede, and their faux versions are now thinner, lighter, and suppler, making them easy to wear in summer or winter. Wools have shifted to tropical weight blends that are fine year-round in all but the most tropical climates.

> I keep saying rules are over... any fabric goes!

### Look for multipurpose basics that use combos of fabrics in the same piece.

For example, a jacket may have faux leather sleeves and a structured wool-blend body (corporate enough for even serious workplaces but datey enough for evenings out), or classic shoes may have cap toes in metallic to tweak the day into night versatility.

### Mix more "glitzy" pieces with your basics when the situation or day is appropriate.

You might wear a sequin tank with a suit or layer a silk cocktail dress under a pullover so the skirt part shows for work.

mesh on anything from a sweater to a skirt. If you don't like color (and still live mostly in black) and don't like prints (at all, no matter what!), go for texture. It will lift a monochromatic, 24/7 wardrobe to the next level and give it style. Don't be defensive about this, either. Some legendary fashion icons lived in black or white and made the shape and proportions of their clothes and accessories and the texture mix the focal point. Here are some of my top texture tips to keep in mind when working more texture into your 24/7 lifestyle.

## Choose light- to medium-weight fabrics to wear solo or layer any day of the year.

Keep this in mind when buying new pieces that may have eye appeal but limited wear. Blends of natural and natural/synthetic fibers and jerseys offer year-round use and comfort. Look for silk/cotton and silk/cashmeres, super-light stretch wools, and viscose/rayon blends.

## Mix textures to give your clothes a split personality.

Combining "masculine" or tough fabrics like leather, tweeds, cords, and flannel with "feminine" ones like eyelet, lace, voile, and silk gives 24/7 wardrobe versatility.

## Rethink your layering technique for style and to open up more 24/7 wear possibilities.

Sheer, super-thin blouses, tees, and tanks can provide a constant base. Summery dresses can get extra warmth worn with sweaters, tights, and boots, and sleeveless tailored dresses can get cozy with a long-sleeve bodysuit or tee under them. Pair those denim, chambray, and flannel shirts you used to consider casual with tailored skirts and suits, or slip satin and silk blouses under ordinary sweaters so the collar, cuff, and tails add a hint of sheen and texture.

# PATTERN

Mixing prints with solid pieces or prints with prints can trend up any 24/7 wardrobe. Don't be afraid to wear prints. Lots of girls think they are "fattening," but it's not true if you follow these tips: Keep the background color dark, or the contrast between print and background low, and the scale of the print small. This works for petite girls who are afraid of prints "overpowering" them and curvy girls who are worried that a generous shape will distort or amplify prints. You can mix prints together too. Just stick to small patterns, one color group (either pastels, warm naturals, brights, or non-colors), and keep one color running throughout your outfit as a theme to hold everything together. You could wear a mixed-pastel floral skirt with some mint green in it with a mint green silk dotted blouse and a two-tone mint cardigan piped in black. Still worried? Here are four more tricks to get prints working for you successfully.

### Wear a print on the better half of your body or in a dress.

An all-over small-scale print that's fluid—meaning it keeps the eye moving—actually hides extra pounds and jiggles. You'll find them in abstracts, floral, squiggly vine or artsy patterns, paisleys on dresses, ankle-cropped pants, silk blouses, and even jeans.

## Don't be afraid to wear prints!

### Wear prints in accessories like scarves, bangles, and bags.

You won't feel like you're overinvesting and overspending if you honestly prefer solids and still get the benefits prints add to a wardrobe.

### Wear animal prints.

Some girls who won't go anywhere near other prints love the look of leopard, zebra, and cheetah. They're easy to wear and work with any of the four style groups depending on the item. Take leopard print as an example. Weekend Girls may love a leopard tank or scarf, Girly Girls may love leopard in stilettos or a cardigan, Sophisticated Girls may wear leopard as a pencil skirt or trench coat, and Sexy Girls may wear a leopard sheath, leopard bras and thongs, or over-the-knee boots.

# THE GRETTA STYLE-OVER

As a working mom, Mika is a true 24/7 multitasker, but her wardrobe didn't reflect that. I suggested she invest in a few tailored pieces like the jacket and straight pants she wears here to carry her from day to night, work week to special events. She can trade the jacket for a silky blouse and the pumps for strappy sandals, or wear the blazer with jeans or over a slim skirt. Navy provides a seasonless color theme and is more unexpected than black.

*before*

*after*

# CHAPTER 3

# WHIP UP A WORKING WARDROBE

WHERE YOU WORK and the kind of work you do influence what you wear no matter what your style. We've been concentrating in the first two chapters on how you see yourself and how your new blueprint for style will boost your confidence and simplify your 24/7 multitasking life. This chapter is all about how others see you. Now it's up to you to make your new style work to your advantage on the job. Successful Girls always want to make more money, move up, get a better job, or enhance their career goals ASAP, and clothes play a starring role. Work is like an audition. You may have all the skills and knowledge necessary to do the job, but you also need to look the part to be taken seriously and get it!

You may even have to modify your look by focusing on certain items from your wardrobe to achieve your goals. Your presentation has to send the right message . . . and stay consistent. You're not off the hook once you make it either. Even in the most senior positions, how you dress is a conscious, controlled decision. The right clothes and accessories let others know they can trust you. Dressing in a way that's too extreme or that reveals too much skin sends the wrong message to colleagues, coworkers, employers, customers, and clients.

My mantra has always been dress for the job you want next, not the one you have. You need to make smart clothing choices to fit in and become part of the team. This is true whether you're an assistant or manager, a new employee, or have worked for the company for years. The secret is to do it without giving up your style.

Opposites attract when it comes to clothes. If your work style and cut are classic, you can get trendier with color and texture. If your work style is trendier in style and cut, go classic and neutral in color.

> *My mantra has always been dress for the job you want next, not the one you have.*

# THE GOTTA-HAVES

**This is your kit for work success**

WHETHER YOU'RE INTERVIEWING FOR A JOB, JUST LANDED ONE, ARE GOING FOR A PROMOTION, OR JUMPING INTO A BRAND-NEW CAREER, THESE TEN GOTTA-HAVES GIVE EVERY GIRL THE EXTRA EDGE. THEY PROVIDE THE RIGHT BALANCE OF STYLE AND AUTHORITY. YOU WANT OTHERS TO SEE YOU AS A FAST-TRACK STAR WORTH WATCHING AND INVESTING IN. USE MY WORK-WORTHY INGREDIENT LIST AS A GUIDE TO SELECTING THE RIGHT PIECES WHILE STICKING TO YOUR LOOK. FOR EXAMPLE, A SUIT IS THE FIRST GOTTA-HAVE, BUT THAT SUIT WILL VARY FOR WEEKEND, GIRLY, SOPHISTICATED, AND SEXY GIRLS. A WEEKEND GIRL SUIT MIGHT MEAN A KNIT BLAZER AND SKIRT, AND A GIRLY GIRL SUIT MIGHT WEAR A DRESS AND JACKET. A SOPHISTICATED GIRL MAY PREFER A TAILORED PANTSUIT, AND A SEXY GIRL MIGHT GO FOR A SHRUNKEN JACKET AND FITTED PANTS. YOU MAY NOT HAVE ALL TEN OF THESE ESSENTIAL FIVE-STAR INGREDIENTS RIGHT THIS MINUTE, BUT THAT'S OK. WORK TOWARD INCLUDING THEM IN YOUR FASHION BATTER AS YOU COOK UP A GOURMET WARDROBE. IT'S ALL PART OF YOUR SUCCESS BLUEPRINT—STAY IN CHARACTER.

## 1. A SUIT

The definition of a suit has expanded way beyond the classic crisp and structured matching top and bottom, although that is still a successful recipe. Suits now may be knits, dress and jacket combos, or unmatched pieces designed that way. All give you an instant put-together feeling of confidence and power. Just be sure the shape and proportions are body skimming for a contemporary fit. Tailor new and old suits to improve the look, customize them to your body, and give them a fresher, pricier appearance. Put together your own unmatched suits from pieces you already own and ramp up your suit style with unexpected accessories like embossed leather booties or a peplum shell in a trendy color.

**BEST CHOICE** If you're buying new, choose a neutral like ivory, black, or navy so both pieces work solo with your other tops and bottoms for maximum flexibility.

## 2. CLOSED-TOE SHOES

Serious work and interview shoes need closed toes. They can be a comfortable, super-low mini-heel to a sexy four inches, platforms or single-sole pumps, or even booties or hybrids like loafer pumps, but they do need closed toes. No Successful Girl wants to worry about a chipped pedicure or a polish that's too wild or trendy. (Save those for after 5 p.m.!) Closed-toe shoes work with bare legs or tights, so they are seasonless. To keep your shoe wardrobe from getting stale, change up your favorite styles with color and texture like patent, snakeskin, suede, or embossed leather. Once you snag the job, peep-toes and even sandals (depending on where you work) are OK, but stay on top of those chips!

**BEST CHOICE** An updated classic pump that's not extreme in height or style so you can bear standing and walking for long hours at a stretch. For example, patent slingbacks with a moderate two-inch heel, platform pumps with a comfy half-inch platform and three inch heel, classic leather stacked heels, or kitten-heel T-straps make sense. It's your call whether you stick to neutrals or spark your shoes with color. You might go for fuchsia suede pumps or low leopard heels to pep up neutral suits and tailored clothes instead of another pair in basic black leather.

## 3. A WORK BAG

This medium to large bag is your traveling office. You want it to look chic and cool but also be classy, lightweight, as slim as possible, and weatherproof. It's where you store everything work-related: tablet, laptop, hard-copy files and documents, pens, notepad, business cards, charger, and glasses. Make sure it's totable by hand or shoulder; versatile straps are an essential feature. The more compartments it has, the easier it is to find things quickly. Of course, you'll want to carry a smaller handbag for personal items too, like your wallet, keys, phone, and makeup. Both bags should be in sync and balance one another in style, look, and proportions. If your hand-carry your work bag, you will want a shoulder bag and vice versa.

**BEST CHOICE** A messenger bag, closed tote, or satchel with dual straps. Some work bags come with (often detachable) wheelies for long commutes, business travel, or presentations, or toting product samples. Neutrals are fine, but color animal prints and metallic finishes can work as standout accent pieces. Look for versions in PVC, microfiber, or hardtop polycarbonate . . . all easy to clean and light.

# 4. A TUNIC-STYLE TOP

Tunics look professional worn over slim pants, a slim skirt, jeans, or leggings on days when you don't want to wear a jacket or dress. They come in every fabric, including crisp woven cotton or linen blends, and knits in cotton, cashmere, or jersey, as well as solids and prints. Choose a body-flattering length that works for you. Most women look best in a tunic that's hip length (especially if you're short) to top of thighs. Boat-necks, crews, or shallow Vs are perfect for work. Wear your tunics straight or belted for more shape.

**BEST CHOICE** A tunic in a color you love (that also works for your wardrobe) that contrasts or tones to any of your slim bottom pieces. For example, if most of your pants and skirts are black, add any black tunic for a monochromatic look, but vary the fabric and neckline—simple tunic sweaters with boat- or V-necks or crisp tunic-shirts with collars and cuffs, for example. Or you can go for contrast and work a black-and-white theme, contrasting white tunic shirts with your black bottom pieces or black-and-white print jersey tunics with black jeans or ankle-cropped pants.

# 5. A SILK BOW BLOUSE

When you want to look authoritative, a sleeveless or sleeved bow blouse has subtle female power and elegance. Bow blouses are one of those used-to-be-retro items that have turned contemporary classic. They have enough wardrobe charisma to let you skip a jacket when worn with a classy pair of straights or a tailored skirt but also work as amazing layering pieces under any cropped jacket or blazer.

**BEST CHOICE** A silky bow blouse in a print, black, or a rich, unexpected color like inky blue or paprika red. Choose a classic high bow for a conservative but ultra-fashionable look or a lower V bow for a slightly sexier and more neck lengthening effect depending on your body proportions and preference. Sleeveless versions don't add any bulk under cardigans or fitted jackets, and long-sleeve styles stand alone as businesslike tops even without a jacket.

## 6. A TOPPER

In fashionese, a topper is a structured, tailored coat. It's easy to wear over dresses, skirts, or pants and won't add bulk to your silhouette. Choose a fit-and-flare princess style, a vintage-inspired A-line, or an updated classic cut straight and slim. Solid colors offer the most versatility, but don't pass up tweeds and metallic-flecked or textured fabrics. They can add personality to work clothes. Neutrals like black, navy, charcoal, or camel are always good bets, but so is a pop-of-color like red, which works for any skin tone.

**BEST CHOICE** A single-breasted tailored coat in a three-quarter or knee length. Choose a three-quarter length for commuting and carpooling if that's part of your routine. This length is easiest to drive in and works with dresses, pants, or jeans for dress-down Fridays or dress-casual workplaces. Knee length is a bit dressier and more formal, but either looks good open or closed, and you can always add a decorative or contrasting belt at the waist for extra style.

## 7. A STATEMENT NECKLACE

When you want people to pay attention to what you say, a chunky collarbone-length necklace or bib necklace that covers slightly more of your upper chest does the trick. Look for eye-catching combos of beads, pearls, chains, and multicolor stones. You can sneak an over-the-top necklace like this into to even the most corporate setting because it doesn't move, clink, or jingle.

**BEST CHOICE** A collarbone-length chunky necklace with an adjustable neckline-friendly clasp.

## 8. A CROPPED JACKET

A short, cropped jacket is the alternative to a fitted blazer. There are two ways to go—feminine styles with an almost retro feel and details like three-quarter bracelet sleeves, soft textured tweed, and bouclé fabrics, or edgier cropped jackets with a military- or biker-inspired cut in tailored wools and cottons, buttery leathers, and knits. Both look great over slim or flared skirts, dresses or jeans, straight pants or slim ankle-cropped styles.

**BEST CHOICE** A single-breasted, three-quarter-sleeve cropped jacket in a textured tweed or buttery leather.

# 9. STRAIGHT-LEG PANTS

Straight-leg pants with a crisp sleek shape are easy to pair with blouses, jackets, and fitted sweaters or tunics. Look for styles that are body skimming with some stretch in the fabric but that are not super-clingy or wide. They go the gamut fabric-wise from relaxed cotton khakis to ponte knits and all-season blends of wool, viscose, and cotton. Look for a mid-rise an inch below the belly button, a flat, non-pleated front, angled pockets that lie flat, and a nice straight drape to the leg so the pants fall straight from hip to hem. They should show your shape but not bag or pull, accent your booty or crotch, or give you camel toe.

**BEST CHOICE** Straights in neutrals like black, navy, tan, or charcoal in a length that works with your favorite work heel height.

# 10. HOSIERY

Some workplaces demand "stockings" all the time and so do some work situations like job interviews, serious meetings, and one-on-ones with your boss. Hosiery is also a quick, inexpensive way to add color or texture to workwear.

**BEST CHOICE** To even out your skin tone if you don't self-tan, choose the sheerest pantyhose you can find and afford in an exact skin tone match, or try small-grid nude fishnets, which do the same thing but are a little sassier. Opaques are practically mandatory for cold-weather wear with all your pumps, flats, and boots. Match tone or go for color, especially if you work in a creative field or fashion-friendly environment. If you wear mostly dark non-colors like black, gray, or navy, tone opaque or textured hose to your clothes for a chic monochromatic look, or add a pop of color with red hose and shoes. If you wear mostly warm, earthy naturals like browns, terra-cotta, olive, rust, and hunter, stay in this color range and tone to match or contrast—

a brown suede skirt with olive tights and booties, for example. If you wear mostly sorbet colors like pale pinks, baby blue, rose, and apricot, stick to nude-look legs. There's nothing worse than pale pastel hose! If you wear mostly brights like red, bold pinks and fuchsia, turquoise, and cobalt, aim for a tone-on-tone look or contrast hose with another bright—a tangerine dress with turquoise tights, for example. To keep the bicolor look sharp and modern, stick to black patent shoes and bags.

# PUSH YOUR PERSONALITY

ONE THING WE'RE NOT DOING: DRESSING TO MIMIC MEN LIKE WOMEN DID IN THE EIGHTIES. YOU DON'T NEED A COOKIE-CUTTER LOOK TO HAVE SUCCESSFUL STYLE AT WORK. IN FACT, LETTING YOUR INDIVIDUALITY SHOW CAN MAKE YOUR WORK STYLE EVEN MORE SUCCESSFUL. NO MATTER HOW MUCH BRAINPOWER, EXPERIENCE, KNOWLEDGE, AND SKILLS YOU BRING TO THE TABLE, YOUR IMPRESSIVE RESUME ISN'T ENOUGH.

An HR manager or business owner wants that first impression when you walk in the door to say it all. As more women take over the workforce (and that includes former stay-at-home moms starting work or returning after a break or maternity leave, college and grad school grads, and those already working part-time but expanding to full-time), we are an impressive group defined more by our diversity than our similarities.

We're deleting stereotypes (and increasing our earning power) by working more in what used to be male-dominated fields like construction, engineering, finance, science, insurance, and medicine, but we still love clothes and makeup. We can do the job but our way...with style. We're taking on careers and trades as veterinarians, chefs, maitre d's, caterers, claims adjusters, factory foremen, accountants and tax examiners, electricians, plumbers, carpenters, psychologists, and health service managers...but we're not giving up on fashion or our looks. More women than men are starting small businesses in the U.S. today, outnumbering guys five to one.

The kind of work you do and where you do it has to be in sync with your clothes preferences even when putting together those 24/7 multitasking uniforms. But having a job and getting the job are two different things.

*Honest truth: If you want a job that pays more, you have to look the part and dress for it.*

# THE OMG! MOMENT

HONEST TRUTH: IF YOU WANT A JOB THAT PAYS MORE, YOU HAVE TO LOOK THE PART AND DRESS FOR IT. EVEN IF YOU'VE BEEN INVESTING IN LEARNING NEW TECHNICAL SKILLS, DOING YOUR RESEARCH, GETTING GREAT JOB REVIEWS, AND NETWORKING LIKE CRAZY, YOU STILL NEED TO STEP UP THE QUALITY OF YOUR CLOTHES.

## Gretta-quette

I'd been appearing on TV as a fashion expert and running my successful fashion and beauty boutiques and spas, but the call to audition for *Tim Gunn's Guide to Style* on Bravo still threw me. I wanted this job and the opportunity to work with Tim (whom I admired and was dazzled by) and his brand. Even with all my own experience as a pro, I agonized over what to wear. Finally, I went with a straight, classic sheath dress in my signature feel-good color, power pink. I had to be sure the fit was perfect, length right at the knee. Then I added patent peep-toe Louboutins, a chunky gold statement necklace, and a quilted Chanel box bag... and got the gig.

Pressure-shopping like this is the worst: You have a job interview or review coming up and you need fresh items (hopefully on sale) immediately. Finding the right pieces, at the right price, at the right time can be like looking for a needle in a haystack.

Lots of girls find themselves in exactly this situation and end up buying the wrong stuff and overspending. Anything on sale in your size with a big-name designer label does not mean it's right for your style, body, or a specific situation like this one. Never buy outside your look just to get a great deal on price. The goal is to upgrade your iconic wardrobe, so don't lose sight of that during sales frenzy. Women usually think they're missing out on something when they shop markdowns or shop in a hurry. Here's a trade secret: Go all the way to the back of the store instead of getting sidetracked by what's new, in the window, or on the mannequin at full price. Hunt for pieces that fit your style, but improve on items you already have in fit, fabric, and workmanship. Look for dresses, jackets, blouses, skirts, and slim, straight pants that can be paired with less costly items you already own to elevate their look.

# THE JOB YOU WANT, THE JOB YOU HAVE, THE JOB YOU NEED

*Keep selling yourself, and don't be shy about your accomplishments and value, especially if you're ready to make a jump.*

## The job you want.

When job-hunting, do your homework before showing up for the interview. This is compulsory whether the position is freelance, part-time, or full-time. It's a requisite whether the job you want is assistant pastry chef, sales associate, claims adjuster, or spa/salon manager. That first impression you make at the interview is what separates you from other applicants. The good news is that there are more women employed in the workforce than ever before in history. The bad news is this also makes it the most competitive time ever in job hunting for women.

Do research on the person or persons you will be meeting with. That may be someone in human resources, your direct manager, or a potential senior colleague. Often more than one person is involved in the hiring process. Find out everything you can about the company, store, or brand before your meeting. Know its current goals, the work environment, and everything possible

about the job itself and the job's responsibilities. If possible, find out discreetly why the position is vacant and what the previous job occupant did or did not do to live up to the requirements. Search online for stats, quotes, or impressive info about the brand, store, or company to slip into your responses. Show in your interview how you can help senior management achieve their goals, and provide answers that show you'll fit in. Demonstrate a super-high level of interest and a desire to do the work with a home-run interview.

Why am I telling you all this in a book on style? Think of your interview as a cupcake—the cake is your perfect

mix of smarts, research, and skills, with the icing providing instant appeal. Delicious as a cupcake may be, if the frosting doesn't do it, you'll pass before even tasting.

To be successful at a job interview, make them think they'd be better off with you than without you. If you turn up looking like you didn't make an effort, forget your sparkling resume. It's over before you open your mouth. Send a positive instant message that you care about this interview and the job and respect your interviewer and the company. Looking unpolished and disorganized in clothes that are too tight, too big, too dated, or put-together

> Looking unpolished and disorganized in clothes that are too tight, too big, too dated, or put-together hit or miss, is not acceptable. Don't take risks.

hit or miss (no matter how expensive they are), is not acceptable. Don't take risks. Make sure your clothes are fresh, pressed, ironed, impeccable, and contemporary. This may mean making an investment buy just for the interview. It may mean calling a friend who wears the same size to borrow an item or two. Wear your best heels and a good-quality bag. Both should be polished, fresh, and unmarred by scuffs, smudges, or stains. If you arrive in flats or weatherproof boots, change your shoes in the lobby or reception area. Do a quick retouch and mirror check in the ladies' room for lint, askew skirt zippers, hair gone awry, and eye makeup smears. Give your teeth a quick brush with a disposable toothbrush, and pop a breath mint. Show them you are there for the job. Look like you can handle the work, the responsibility, and their trust in your success.

Bottom line? If someone shows up for a job interview looking unprepared, the message received is, *If she looks this unprepared for the interview, she's not prepared for work every day either. Pass!*
I should know. I hire people every day and have over 100 employees.

## The job you have.

It's a misconception that once you have the job you don't have to try anymore. Don't ever let go of your style and maintenance routine. Tenure is not a safety net. Don't get lazy about your clothes or complacent about your look. If your job is part-time, don't dress part-time.

Never get too comfy, even if you seem to have supportive, contented colleagues and clients. Be your best self every single day and dress that way. You always have to maintain and demonstrate how valuable you are to the company and your employer. Looking tired, sloppy, rushed, stressed, or not current is not an option. Stay on top of loose buttons and threads, saggy hems, lint (we love our cats and dogs, but they can leave hairs!), creases, stains, and pulls and pilling on sweaters and knits. Make dry-cleaner runs routine, and keep a small emergency sewing kit plus scissors, safety pins, double-faced styling tape, and stain-removal wipes in your desk, car, or work bag.

## The job you need.

Keep selling yourself, and don't be shy about your accomplishments and value, especially if you're ready to make a jump. Always be doing a constant commercial for yourself. Shop online and at sales to upgrade your basics and accessories (more details further on in this chapter), but maintain your style. Stay on top of beauty routines (more on that in chapter 8) so skin, hair, makeup, and nails always look groomed. Maintenance is everything. To make it to the top tier of your company or field or move into a new job, stay competitive. Keep improving your work and look. Be sure everyone—especially those who count—notice and know it. Make a conscious effort to look like a leader every day.

# THE WORK FORMULA FOR STYLE + SUCCESS

THE POWER OF THE RIGHT STYLE AT WORK (AND BEYOND) HAS BEEN DEMONSTRATED IN MOVIES LIKE *WORKING GIRL* (JUST CHECK OUT MELANIE GRIFFITH'S TRANSFORMATION IN THAT FILM!), JULIA ROBERTS IN *PRETTY WOMAN*, BRITTANY MURPHY IN *CLUELESS*, ANNE HATHAWAY IN *THE PRINCESS DIARIES* AND *THE DEVIL WEARS PRADA*, AND SANDRA BULLOCK IN *MISS CONGENIALITY*.

And let's not forget we were raised on *Cinderella*. But there's a difference between a movie makeover and real life.

Each of the four Successful Girl looks has within its style menu plenty of work recipes to suit any job situation and provide a 24/7 uniform. Nailing that initial job interview is the challenge. You don't get a second chance. You need to make a positive first impression to get the job or a callback for a follow-up interview. In order for that to happen, you need to look like you could step into the job that minute. What's on your resume counts, but so does style.

You do need to consider what the actual job is you're applying for when deciding what to wear. If you show up in a suit and pumps for a creative job, it won't get you in the door. Any company, industry, or workplace today expects applicants at every level to look convincing and real.

*Turn the page to see the recipes that every girl needs to make the get a sure thing!*

# IF YOU'RE A
# Weekend Girl

Your style in general is more casual. Although some workplaces have relaxed dress codes with jeans-on-Fridays or a more laid-back look all the time, don't do it for your interview. You might pair a knit jacket—blazer or cropped style—with a knit pencil or straight pants for a suit look. You could also go the dress route in a matte jersey wrap. Both solutions allow you to stay comfortable without sending an off-duty message. You don't want to be underdressed for this meeting.

**INTERVIEW ITEMS TO CONSIDER:**

- A knit blazer or a cropped knit jacket
- A knit or jersey dress
- Knit ankle-cropped or straight pants
- Low or stacked heels or polished dress flats
- A knit straight skirt or a pencil
- A simple, quality leather sling bag
- A tote or shoulder bag
- Gold or silver hoops, a statement pendant with one big stone or charm

# IF YOU'RE A
# Girly Girl

Your overall look is feminine, but for a job interview, don't look too sweet or overdo the girly, romantic theme. You still need to look ready for business. Let your personality come through in embellished pieces, ladylike shapes, and accessories with something extra, but don't overdo the ruffles, frills, and bows. Choose a dress or a skirt plus blouse and cardigan combo (or add a jacket instead), a shoulder bag or satchel with a decorative detail like a bow (not a clutch), and your best pumps, which may be Mary Janes, T-straps, or cap toes.

## INTERVIEW ITEMS TO CONSIDER:

- A tailored sheath or A-line dress
- A tailored skirt that moves (pleats, flippy hem, A-line, trumpet, pencil)
- A silky bow blouse, a draped shell, or peplum top
- An embellished cardigan in a color (stones or sequins at the neckline, for example, or crystal buttons)
- A cropped jacket in a pretty tweed or bouclé, a peplum jacket
- Feminine heels like cap-toe pumps, Mary Janes, or T-straps
- A quilted chain strap bag or an embossed leather or metallic frame bag
- A statement bracelet or necklace with stones and shine

# IF YOU'RE A
# Sophisticated Girl

Your style is polished and updated classic. You never want to look dated or too traditional at a job interview. Pay attention to fresh details so that basics like suits, blazers, cashmere sweaters, and white shirts look current. Add your "secret sauce" with color, proportion, and prints. To stand out, you need to work those classics with a twist. You might wear a navy blue pinstripe pantsuit, but pair it with a printed silk blouse and unexpected shoes like python pumps.

**INTERVIEW ITEMS TO CONSIDER:**

- A fitted skirt-suit or pantsuit, matched or unmatched
- A tailored dress and coat duo
- A tailored pencil skirt
- Silky print blouse or a crisp white shirt

- A structured sheath
- Pumps or boots in embossed leather or quality patent leather
- A contoured belt or narrow patent belt
- Pearls; vintage-look jewelry

# IF YOU'RE A
## Sexy Girl

You're all about female power and fitted body-skimming clothes. You don't want to distract from your resume and presentation by showing too much skin. You can still be sexy in the right way by wearing fitted clothes that cover and show your shape. Too-low necklines, obvious cleavage, or too-short minis don't belong at an interview and make you appear insecure. You might wear a body-confident sheath accented with a belt at the waist and high heels or slim tailored pants with a leather or suede jacket.

**INTERVIEW ITEMS TO CONSIDER:**

- **A tapered pencil skirt**
- **A leopard scarf or blouse**
- **A curve-hugging sheath with a high neckline**
- **A belted jacket**
- **Platform or classic high-heel pumps**

- **Slim tailored pants**
- **A structured bag with hardware—buckles, straps, studs**
- **Chain-link jewelry, a bold cuff bracelet, or mixed long necklaces**

# THE GRETTA STYLE-OVER

KIANNA'S CAREER GOT A FAST-TRACK BOOST FROM POLISHED MAKEUP, A SLEEK BLOWOUT AND A WARDROBE UPGRADE. I SUGGESTED MODERN, TAILORED PIECES IN NEUTRAL COLORS THAT MIX EASILY AND PROVIDE VERSATILITY FOR WORK AND AFTER-FIVE.

*before*

*after*

# CHAPTER 4

# LOVE
# +
# STYLE
# =
# SUCCESS

NOW YOU'VE GOT YOUR OWN STYLE and personalized formulas to navigate a 24/7 lifestyle and work. Time to get up close and personal because the right clothes can bring success into your relationships too. Let's start with a key question. Where are you on the love spectrum right this minute? You may be single, divorced, just getting back into dating, looking for romance, or halfway to falling in love. The right clothes can help you attract the right relationships and seal the deal on ones in progress. If you're part of a newly committed couple, in a long-term relationship, or mar-

or fourteen. It doesn't matter whether you're curvy like Sofia Vergara or Kim Kardashian, pencil slim like Anne Hathaway or Keira Knightley, or fit and muscle-toned like Michelle Obama or Madonna—the Successful Girl knows looking and feeling confident makes all the difference when it comes to love and style.

Let's establish that looking a certain kind of sexy is absolutely OK. As my soul mate, Ricky, says, "Guys want to see what we're dealing with. The fewer surprises later on, the better." That said, I'm going to immediately remind you that staying sexy is for *you* first, the other person second. It's not about getting a guy or dressing to please someone else's taste or fantasy. You are simply choosing to reveal another side of you. Attracting positive attention provides incentive to continue making "me" time for maintenance and updates in your look and style. In fact, the

*Let's establish that looking a certain kind of sexy is absolutely OK.*

ried, what you wear can keep the flame going.

The secret to success in love is to never let go of your hot-girl self. Even though you have a terrific personality, intelligence, integrity, and a warm, caring attitude, don't underestimate the value of sex appeal. Maintaining that part of you is crucial whether you're establishing a new connection or reheating an existing one. Hotness, FYI, is not about being a certain size, having a perfect body, or looking like a fashion model or celebrity. Certain style recipes I'm going to share with you are foolproof whether you're a size four

single most important take-away from this chapter is to never let yourself go in terms of looks and style whatever your relationship status. Some women gain extra weight or slack off on healthy eating habits that impact looks. Others neglect their appearance or lose interest in clothes between relationships or when the romance cools or becomes comfortably routine. Carving out daily, weekly, and monthly time for your looks and maintenance is how to stay successful in love, healthy in your attitude, and sexy.

# THE GOTTA-HAVES

**This is your love kit for success**

When you're out there looking, what you wear is an essential part of the Successful Girl's initial meet-and-greet strategy. Successful attraction is all about knowing how much to show and how to body-brag without grandstanding or under-advertising. You can't display too much, and you can't trot out too little. The initial reaction you create is within your control and certain items are Gretta-guaranteed love magnets.

These ten items are all about flaunting you in a good way. We all need a little help when it comes to successfully getting the right kind of attention from the right person. You don't need trickery, like lots of extra padding to boost your boobs and booty, and you don't need to add lots of extra makeup and perfume either. (Guys say it's a turnoff.) You'll notice I've listed several different kinds of tops and footwear here, and for a very good reason. Lots of girls who live a 24/7 lifestyle—no matter what their fashion style—can work the simple formula of fitted sexy jeans as a base plus flirtatious tops and heels. This list also gives you other options.

## 1. A SHEER TOP

A blouse that is loose, flowy, and feminine is my first go-to. It may be silk, chiffon, lace, or a combo of soft fabrics, and it may be have sleeves or be sleeveless, or be a blouson, peplum, or tiered tank, but it has to float and move. That's the subtle seductive element here.

**BEST CHOICE** A sheer black button-down blouse over an opaque black tank, camisole, or bodysuit suits every style.

## 2. A MAJOR BLACK LEATHER PIECE THAT'S NOT A JACKET

This can be a slim cropped pant, jeans, leggings, a pencil skirt, or a sleeveless sheath dress or shift. It may even be a combo knit and leather with stretch panel inserts instead of all leather, or faux leather, but it's a modern way of saying sexy.

**BEST CHOICE** A sleeveless high-neck sheath with or without stretch panel inserts is a new classic piece that's great solo, belted, or under a cardigan or jacket.

# 3. A BODY-SKIMMING FITTED DRESS

Show your shape, not your skin! Choose from jerseys and knits or tailored sheaths in your best above-the-knee length. This can be anywhere from just above to a few inches higher, but skip fitted minis. Look for a neckline that flatters without showing too much chest (like a wide V or scoop) and draping or ruching for camouflage detailing.

**BEST CHOICE** A sheath that shows your best, be it toned arms, a beautiful decolletage (not too low though!) or a trim waist.

# 4. A SHOULDER-BARING TOP

This can be a halter, off-shoulder, one-shoulder asymmetric, strapless, or scooped-out cold-shoulder top with sleeves, but it's a foolproof date-night item.

**BEST CHOICE** A one-shoulder asymmetric top flatters all—from a small bust to a full chest—and shows shoulders without revealing cleavage crack. You can wear it to work under a blazer and take it off after 5 p.m. for drinks.

# 7. STRAPPY SHOES

Show your beautifully groomed feet and a fabulous pedicure in some sort of open or sandaly shoe—from a cage bootie to ankle straps or even peep toes.

**BEST CHOICE** A sexy high-heel sandal if you have great feet or slingback heels if you really don't.

# 8. A FITTED KNEE-HIGH BOOT

A tall leg-clinging boot in a supple stretch fabric. This can be stretch leather or stretch suede, boots with a stretch panel, or even a microfiber stretch boot. The boot should fit like a second skin—no gaps or thick, stiff, chunky styles—and it should hit your leg just under the knee.

**BEST CHOICE** An elegant, tapered-toe black stretch leather boot with a high heel.

## 5. A SPARKLY TOP

Any shimmery top sends a dressed-up message. It can be subtle as in a metallic shell or a stone-studded neckline, or blatantly glam as in a sequin-covered tee. It dresses up work clothes or jeans fast and requires no extra jewelry for glitz.

**BEST CHOICE** A knit sequin-covered tank or tee. It swaps in easily and can stay on standby in a tote, desk, or car for last-minute invites. Choose black, white, gold, or silver.

## 6. DELICATE JEWELRY THAT MOVES

You want earrings, bracelets, and necklaces that sway and shift slightly as you gesture, turn your head, or change body stance. First of all, they're flirtatious, and second, they call attention to you and every little move you make. Filigree cuffs and earrings with a lacey look are also good picks.

**BEST CHOICE** A dangly earring or hoops that

shine or sparkle. Choose a pair that contrast with your hair color so they show in long hair as you toss your head. Glam earrings won't compete with shine and glitz in your clothes if you stick to one piece of clothing with shimmer.

## 9. A FITTED ANKLE BOOT WITH A HEEL

These should hug the leg and foot and can also be a stretch leather or suede and work as an edgier alternative to a classic pump.

**BEST CHOICE** Just above the ankle booties with a "collar" that extends past the ankle bone if your legs are toned, shapely, or slim, or a lower cut bootie—in a V-shape—that dips in front to hit the metatarsal bone at your instep for those with heavy ankles and calves.

## 10. SKINNY JEANS

Before you say no, ask any guy. A perfectly fitted skinny jean is a step up from leggings, and the sturdier stretch fabric holds and molds to your contours and plays up your booty, which is fine. Skinny jeans are actually a big range from straight cigarette legs to extreme body-hugging styles that cling like pantyhose.

**BEST CHOICE** A medium nine-inch rise, dark stretch-denim that fits like a second skin and follows your shape from waist to ankle looks great tucked into tall boots, with booties, or with strappy sandals.

# THE OMG! MOMENT

No matter what your personal style—Weekend, Girly, Sophisticated or Sexy—Successful Girls know relationships require work and strategy, not just passion. Same with clothes. You can't just wear the same old and expect fresh results. We're all either looking for love, spicing up the relationship we have, or rebounding (and relaunching) our hot selves back into the dating world. Applying the same tactics you learned in chapters 1 through 3 work here as well. This means checking your inspiration board and maybe adding to it with specific pieces and accessories that are flirtatious, romantic, or sensual.

## STYLE CAN MAINTAIN YOUR MOJO

Here's the reality: You have about ten seconds to establish chemistry when meeting someone new or approaching someone you already know in a date-possible way. You want to put your best self forward by confidently highlighting your assets. The Successful Girl is always on-call when it comes to new relationship possibilities. Spontaneity sounds great, but planning for it is the smartest approach. Don't rush out and shop for something new just because you're ready to take an online match to an in-person level or because friends have suggested a fix-up. Check your inspiration board first. You may have pieces that fit the gotta-haves listed above. The venue and timing count, of course, so being prepared with a few items to swap into your 24/7 work formula are a good idea. You don't want to show up in a turtleneck and flats or your oldest jeans and baggy layers that don't show your shape.

No pressure, but you do need to give dating looks additional thought. They'll differ according to your style.

*The Successful Girl is always on-call when it comes to new relationship possibilities. Spontaneity sounds great, but planning for it is the smartest approach.*

### Looking for love.

You're free and ready, so it's time to reboot your hot-girl look. Don't get stuck in a comfort zone of everyday clothes. Your 24/7 and work formulas will continue to evolve as you gain confidence in your style. You may even find yourself blurring the boundaries a bit as you explore new trends and ideas. But right now, what you need to do is find the special pieces within your look that add sizzle. You want your style to stay consistent and send the right message but still feel like you. Let's take that body-skimming dress on the gotta-have list for example. A Girly Girl would never feel comfortable going on a romantic dinner date in a black leather sheath, and a Sexy Girl would never feel like herself in a draped pink silk one. A Sophisticated Girl would be sending the wrong message by wearing a ruched, jersey zebra print, and a Weekend Girl would be misleading herself and potential partners in a crisp, tailored style. Your clothes are the invitation to your life.

### Spicing up what you have.

You can get stuck in a rut in a relationship, but pumping up your style can help pull you out. The idea of being with someone who thinks we look beautiful without makeup and in our PJs is appealing, but be careful. Losing touch with that routine of "getting ready" can also make you lose touch with your hot-girl side. Rebooting your mojo with racy unexpected pieces like a silky nightie or short, silk kimono instead of a big tee or fuzzy robe at home or slipping a lacy corset under your top instead of your usual nude bra can restore a first-date glow.

### The rebounding breakover.

We've all been there. It's over, and you need to start fresh. Maybe you've been dumped or decided yourself to end a marriage or leave a relationship. Maybe you've been alone by choice—focusing on your career, spending time with your kids as a single mom, or getting through a drawn-out divorce. Give yourself time to heal. The Successful Girl needs to reconnect to herself before relaunching a dating life and her style. Getting to a place where you can leave anger, sadness, and depression behind and move on is a priority. When you do, it's time to find someone who will love you for your true self. That's why your date look has to be truly you in spirit and reveal what makes you … you! Your new style blueprint is once again going to be your guide. No more wearing what looks sexy on someone else or the old you, and certainly not what your former partner liked! Your most alluring look is your brand-new style. Check out the stylish celebs who did a "breakover" like Katie Holmes, Amy Poehler, Minka Kelly, and Heidi Klum. Own it! Don't be a re-Gretta!

# THE **Weekend Girl** ON "DATE" NIGHT MIGHT WEAR

Jeweled ballet flats and flip flops, floaty drape-y neck tees and tunics, and a soft foldover clutch or a cross-body mini bag are also great options and easy to find at every price.

Vintage-wash skinnies
+ an off-the-shoulder floaty top
+ strappy wedges
+ dangly beaded earrings

Fitted ankle-cropped jeans
+ a printed silk halter top
+ suede booties
+ a stack of sliver-thin silver bangles

# THE **Girly Girl** ON "DATE" NIGHT MIGHT WEAR

*or*

Tops or dresses in fabrics like eyelet, lace or crochet, vintage look, prints and trims, or extra details like embroidery, bows, piping, or beading, send your message loud and clear.

**Pastel jeans**
+ a peplum blouse
+ strappy embellished heels
+ sparkly crystal hoops

**Floral print jeans**
+ a draped jersey top
+ a colorful, jeweled shoe-bootie
+ a lariat necklace

# THE **Sophisticated Girl** ON "DATE" NIGHT MIGHT WEAR

Select discreet spots to reveal with low backs, peek-a-boo shoulders, and keyhole necklines instead of the obvious.

**Black fitted jeans**
+ a silk blouse
+ knee-high black stretch boots
+ long ropes of pearls or delicate chains studded with stones

*or*

**Dark denim skinnies**
+ a wrap jersey top
+ a charm bracelet

# THE **Sexy Girl** ON "DATE" NIGHT MIGHT WEAR

*or*

Play up legs or cleavage, not both, and use accessories like long, layered necklaces, and attention-getting shoes and booties to highlight your assets. Stay strategic (sex-tregic).

**Leather jeans**
+ a one-shoulder asymmetric top
+ fringed stiletto booties
+ dangly line earrings that sparkle

**White jeans**
+ gold strappy heels
+ off-shoulder knit top
+ gold cuff

# SHOW YOU CARE. SHOW YOU'RE A SUCCESS.

THIS IS NOT THE TIME TO BE COY OR HESITANT. YOUR STYLE CAN WELCOME SOMEONE INTO YOUR LIFE OR SEND THEM IN THE OTHER DIRECTION. IT'S A POWERFUL TOOL AND TOTALLY IN YOUR CONTROL. YOUR CHOICE OF CLOTHES AND HOW TO PUT THEM TOGETHER EXPRESS YOUR TASTE, SELF-ESTEEM, AND EASE WITH YOUR BODY AND PEOPLE. WHETHER THIS IS A FIRST DATE, SECOND, OR SOMEWHERE ON YOUR WAY TO HAVING A RELATIONSHIP, FOLLOW THESE TIPS.

## Use positive body language.

Clothes alone can't do all the work. How you sit, stand, and walk in them is part of the positive package you present. Slouching is a common mistake girls make, especially when we're off-duty, having a cocktail or two, or relaxed and in a comfortable, intimate setting like a restaurant, bar, or cafe. Slouchy posture makes you look heavier, flabbier, shorter, and less confident in your attitude. Make a conscious effort to pull your shoulders back and straighten up, but not stiffly. Think of dancers, models, and actors and how they use their bodies to communicate poise and casual elegance.

Make contact—eye and physical. Don't be afraid to use subtle touches on the arm or shoulder as you tell a story, and do a double kiss when greeting someone. If a woman leans in from the first hello and makes eye contact, she takes charge of the situation. When you're in a crowd (at a party or event for example) and mingling and meeting a lot of people, it's up to the Successful Girl to establish an intimate connection in those ten seconds we discussed. Rent the movies *How to Lose a Guy in 10 Days* with Kate Hudson, *Bridget Jones's Diary*, *Amélie*, and *When Harry Met Sally* for inspiration!

## Wear home-run colors to warm things up.

There have been several psychological studies, including one published in 2012 by the University of Rochester, proving that red is the most alluring color to wear…more so than any other color. Just confirming what we already knew, which is why red lipstick and nail polish are classics! And red, FYI, is not one color but a rainbow of hues from scarlet to tomato to deep rosy red. The runner-up in my opinion? Power pink! A hot, bright pink makes a feminine but pretty fierce statement too and flatters every skin tone. Wearing a bold, bright color quickly shows you have a sense of fun, personality, and spirit, which is important one-on-one but also crucial when meeting his friends and family. What if you're more into pastels or neutrals? Add color in your accessories. Even tiny, brilliantly hued stones on a necklace or earrings, or a colorful shoe or bag, can add sizzle. Give your Little Black Dress a break.

## Check your expectations and the venue.

Keep in mind that the person you're really out to please is yourself when it comes to style and romance. No need to update your Facebook relationship status if you get beyond date one or hit the sales for a shopping spree. You never want your brain to race from date to boyfriend, soul mate, or father of my baby in a few hours or change your style to suit his. The Successful Girl dresses for dating with a knowing attitude and self-assurance. If you're true to yourself, you'll be attracting partners with similar tastes or at least those you find appealing. If you haven't a clue whether to go low-key or dress up, the Love gotta-have jeans+ formula keeps you covered and lets him know you made an effort. It'll get you through almost any situation, from neighborhood bar to urban club to a movie, dinner, or concert. You can also dial down a fitted dress or pencil skirt by adding a vest (fur, military/safari inspired, puffer) or a jean jacket and booties.

## Know what's a turn-off and do yourself a favor.

Avoid certain items that send the wrong message even if you love them. Don't wear anything too revealing (guys like the slow show) or too covered (a turtleneck). Avoid carrying a gigantic bag no matter how chic. It makes him think you need a support staff of makeup, hair, and emergency items and are high-maintenance. If you're coming straight from work to a restaurant or party, check your big bag and carry a small one with essentials. Don't wear something ridiculously trendy like super-clunky shoes or something suspiciously camouflagey like an empire dress or top (could be maternity wear) or a hat.

Have with you Tylenol or Advil for stress headaches, cash, a credit card (expect to pay your half), breath mints, tissues, a phone charger in case your phone dies (so you can call a cab, navigate home), minty lip balm so your chapped dry kisser stays soft, and a mini disposable toothbrush for post-dinner/coffee freshening.

## Gretta-quette

I met the father of my son, Kai, for the first time very briefly at an event. Each of us had been told about the other by mutual friends. I describe it as an emotional collision! I was beautifully dressed in a floor-length Missoni tank-style dress that revealed my shape. Our first real date, though, was during the summer at a casual downtown Mexican restaurant in NYC. Ricky suggested I "dress comfortably" since we planned on walking around the neighborhood following dinner. As a Girly Girl, all I really wanted to do was dress up! I ended up wearing a very successfully sexy look without giving up my own feminine style: fitted jeans, wedge sandals, a sheer flowy top with a lacy tank beneath, light strands of silvery jewelry, and thin hoops, and I left my hair wavy for a feminine, tousled look. It's been one of my favorite go-to looks ever since.

# GRETTA'S SEXY SECRET

Every girl thinks a guy expects a Victoria's Secret model to pop out of her clothes when things get racy. Let me clear up any confusion or misconceptions about this for you. He's more turned on by the hot you than any stereotypical image. All you need to do is be prepared for those fun sexy moments with clothes and lingerie that make seduction easy.

Don't let weight, size, or the concept of a guy judging you cloud your self-confidence and get in your way. You have an appreciative audience, and you are the star. Success in the bedroom is all about mood, ambiance, environment, and style.

Make sensual lingerie, music, lighting, and fresh linens with a hint of lavender spray a habit. It's all part of setting the stage. Make sure your lingerie is beautiful—no rips, tears, snares, pilling, or pulls. Style up the romance by not wearing shapewear "shorts" on a night you think may turn intimate (too girdly) though pretty, glamorous shapewear slips are fine. No to sports bras (not sexy) and granny panties (so not sexy!). Skip anything complicated to get into and out of, like button-fly jeans and items with lots of buckles to undo or tricky hook-and-eye closures.

## Gretta's Lingerie Kit

**A BALCONY BRA**
Also called a balconette or demi-bra. This is essentially an underwire bra with a half-cup shape so the top of your boobs are exposed and projected. Due to the shape, the straps are widely spaced, making this a great bra to wear with square, scoop, or open necklines.

**A PLUNGE BRA**
This deeply V'd bra fastens low in front, making it a good choice for super V-necks or button-front shirts and blouses. More discreet than the push-up, it doesn't push your breasts up and together; it just allows a peek.

**A PUSH-UP BRA**
When you want to maximize cleavage and hike up the girls, this is the go-to.

**Here's how a dating wardrobe can be a success and where it flops.**

**THE GIRL WHO KNOWS TOO MUCH** overdoes the sex appeal by going for extreme statements in every item she wears. She's obvious and cheesy and ends up alone or with the wrong kind of attention. She may even look too high-maintenance for most. She wears zebra-print leggings; big, dangly, chandelier earrings; a huge cocktail ring and a necklace with bling; a double-V deeply revealing Lurex knit top; foot-squeezing peep-toe pumps with toe cleavage, in attention-demanding red patent; lots of extra hair extensions with highlights; bright, glossy lipstick; and long nails with glitzy nail art, and she carries a gold shoulder bag with decorative key chain and charms.

**THE GIRL WHO KNOWS TOO LITTLE** thinks she's fine with her usual, 24/7 look and never makes the extra effort. She wears comfy cargos and loafer flats. a boxy crew-neck sweater layered over a cotton tank and striped shirt, mascara and lip gloss, second-day hair in a braid, reading glasses, and chipped nail polish, and she carries a huge bag with an extra jean jacket and scarf.

**THE SUCCESSFUL GIRL** gets it right! She is wearing a stretch-leather pencil skirt; a silky wrap blouse; killer, sexy, cage booties; fluid, light, dangly, chain necklaces; fresh, bouncy, shiny hair; and defined eyes and lips in neutral colors, and she is carrying her favorite python box clutch.

**THONGS AND G-STRINGS**
A low-rise version of these disappears under clothes and makes panty lines history.

**DEMI-BRIEFS AND BIKINIS**
If you have more booty, these give you a cheeky look with a little more coverage. Look for those cut high at the thigh, not straight across like boy shorts, to slim and elongate your legs.

**FISHNETS AND SEXY HOSE**
Fine-mesh fishnets, thigh-highs, lacy tights, and sheer black pantyhose are all "special" items with a mission.

**A CORSET**
Sometimes retro-inspired shapewear can be alluring. Look for feminine, lacy, silky versions meant for play.

after

# THE GRETTA STYLE-OVER

CHRISTIE WAS READY FOR ROMANCE AGAIN WHEN WE MET AFTER SHE SPENT A DECADE RAISING HER CHILDREN TO ADULTHOOD AS A 9/11 WIDOW. HER WARDROBE WAS BASIC, PRACTICAL, BUT BLAH. I INSPIRED HER TO REBOOT HER STYLE WITH SOPHISTICATED FEMININE CHOICES THAT PLAY UP HER SHAPE. THIS RED PEPLUM DRESS GOES FROM OFFICE TO COCKTAILS WITH JUST A CHANGE OF SHOES.

before

# CHAPTER 5

# AGE
# +
# STYLE
# =
# SUCCESS

THE TERM "AGE APPROPRIATE" can sound outdated when women of every age are sharing identical looks, trends, and style. When women twenty-five to fifty-five shop the same stores, buy the same brands, and put clothes together in a similar contemporary way, they seem to look ageless. Look at celeb mom-daughters like Goldie Hawn and Kate Hudson, Madonna and Lourdes, Christie Brinkley and Alexa Ray Joel, or Peggy Lipton and Rashida Jones who often wear alike looks, and the fashion boundaries get pretty blurry.

But look more closely and you'll see that Successful Girls at every age are being more clever about manipulating style to their advantage without a list of shoulds and should-nots. Sometimes younger women want their clothes to not only play up their style but to also help them to be taken seriously. They want to appear more experienced, knowledgeable, skilled, competent, reliable, and trustworthy, especially when an interview, job, client, assignment, apartment, or bank loan hangs in the balance. Older women are working, dating, and wanting to be viewed as informed, up to date, technologically competent, contemporary, open to new ideas, and even sexy. They also want to get the interview, job, client, assignment, or possibly a date and realize dialing their style up or down is the way to go. Younger women do not need to limit their fashion choices to only the most classic, conservative pieces, and older women do not have to go trendy as a supermodel either.

The secret to wearing what you like at every age is knowing how to manipulate your clothes to achieve your goals. If you keep updating your inspiration board and checklist, you'll still have plenty of wiggle room to experiment, blend in new items, stay true to your style, and look ageless in a good way. The difference between the old you and the Successful Girl you are now is your blueprint, which will continue to guide you.

Looking seasoned, competent, and well dressed is smart no matter what your age when your goals have a serious edge that includes work, finances, or legal matters. Your clothes have to help project confidence in your decision-making abilities and judgment and dial up your professional look. This is not the time to break out the trendy mini shorts or your see-through chiffon blouse ... but a metallic-tweed pencil skirt and fresh white silk blouse? Yes! On the other hand, when you want to make an impression as fresh, energetic, creative, progressive, and savvy, this is the ideal time to add an edge to your favorite tailored 24/7 dress or black pants and sweater with a fitted cropped jacket in a trendy color and the hottest shoes or booties around.

The age issue is not whether to get into trends; the issue is how far to trend up. A lot depends on your taste, body, lifestyle, and your personal style. As CEO of your look, you need to ask some questions: Does it fit my style blueprint? If so, will it work with what I own? Every new seasonal "buy" is a business decision, and you need to consider the short-term and long-term benefits.

> *Looking seasoned, competent, and well dressed is smart no matter what your age.*

# THE GOTTA-HAVES

**This is your no-age kit for success**

AGE IS ONLY RELEVANT WHEN YOUR CLOTHES CHOICES DON'T ENHANCE YOUR LOOKS OR HELP YOUR STYLE. BY THE TIME YOU READ THIS CHAPTER, YOU'VE DISCOVERED HOW IDENTIFYING AND STICKING TO YOU ICONIC LOOK CAN BOOST YOUR CONFIDENCE, INCREASE THE VERSATILITY OF YOUR CLOTHES, ELEVATE YOUR WORK LOOK, AND ENHANCE YOUR MOJO. NOW LEARN HOW TO MANIPULATE THAT LOOK TO CREATE THE AGELESS LOOK YOU WANT TO PROJECT. THE WAY YOU PUT YOUR WARDROBE PIECES TOGETHER CAN HELP DIAL UP SOPHISTICATION AND EXPERIENCE OR DIAL DOWN FOR A MORE YOUTHFUL EFFECT. THIS IS HOW THE SUCCESSFUL GIRL NEVER LETS THE DATE ON HER DRIVER'S LICENSE GET IN THE WAY OF HER GOALS.

## 1. A CASHMERE SWEATER

There's something very chic about a cashmere sweater that makes it an age-free essential. Go with your look and preference: a relaxed sweatshirt style or cashmere tee in soothing gray for Weekend Girls, a ballet-neck scoop in rose or pale bisque for a Girly Girl, a fitted crew- or boat-neck in navy or ivory for a Sophisticated Girl, and a deep V in black for a Sexy Girl.

**BEST CHOICE** A style and color that will boost your multitasking life and can be worn solo or layered, dressed up or down for any season.

## 2. A PENCIL SKIRT

A straight tapered skirt can look chic and cool or classy and elegant depending on the fit, fabric, and length. Designers work them into every season no matter what else is happening on the runway. There are options that suit every Successful Girl's style, including tweeds, leather, prints, sequins, and knits in addition to the traditional suiting fabrics and neutrals in gabardine, twill, cotton, and rayon.

**BEST CHOICE** A flat-front, back zip, no-pocket, no waistband, knee-grazing or just-above style that lies smoothly over hips, tummy, and derriere without pulling.

## 3. A NEW WHITE TEE, COTTON SHIRT, OR SILK BLOUSE

A white top lights up your skin and makes you look wide-awake, rested, and fresh even when you're not. It also sends a message of "new" to anything you pair it with.

**BEST CHOICE** There really are three white basics here that work for any style and perk up your wardrobe fast. Consider a white silk shirt that drapes elegantly and flows over curves, a crisp white cotton shirt that's shaped to your contours (not a boxy man-style fit!), and a classic white tee with a little stretch and opaque enough so you can't see your bra (wear a no-nipple T-shirt bra).

## 4. A LEATHER STATEMENT JACKET

Real or faux leather in a biker-inspired, ladylike cropped, or buttery tailored jacket makes every girl look edgy, sexy, and expensive in a modern way. The texture should be soft and the cut clean—no overkill on the details. Go for the simplest style in your most flattering cut and shape.

**BEST CHOICE** Black and tailored to work over dresses, work pants, and jeans. Dial it up with silk blouse, pencil skirt, booties, or cage shoes. Dial it down with a tee and cargos or a sweaterdress and flat boots.

## 7. COOL GLASSES

Real Rx glasses (the kind you need to see the fine print, a movie, computer screen, or drive) and even fashion glasses with clear lenses have become major fashion accessories. Lately, big, strong, nerd styles in black, tortoise, or funky colors and big cat-eye frames give everyone a fashionable look. These look-at-me frames work for all.

**BEST CHOICE** Big, black, bold, masculine-looking frames work for every face and add definition even when you're not wearing makeup. They project a combo of style and intelligence that can't miss.

## 8. COLOR JEANS

Get out of the basic-blue rut with clear fruit and jelly-bean-color jeans in a skinny, ankle-cropped stretch fabric or a clingier jegging. They look modern and energize all your basic black and white tops and jackets.

**BEST CHOICE** Red jeans give your entire closet a lift. It's a power color that instantly takes a plain white tee or black blazer into a trendier look without a lot of fuss.

## 5. AN EXOTIC SKIN BAG

Any bag gets a lift from a skin or fabric with texture or pattern. Embossed leathers that look like croc or ostrich, snakeskin, stamped calf hair with a cheetah or zebra pattern, and fabric bags printed for an exotic-skin look are always hot and add just enough fashion to even the most classic outfits.

**BEST CHOICE** A large satchel, soft shoulder bag, or clutch in any color from ombré blue snakeskin to metallic mock croc. Make it an everyday statement or date-night accent.

## 6. SHIFT DRESS

This straight or A-line structured dress is sleeveless and at its most versatile and wearable for everyone with a collarbone-skimming shallow-scoop neckline. Designers never stop making new variations, and sixties mod style and icons like Jackie O made it a year-round staple.

**BEST CHOICE** A black, sleek shift in an all-season modal/poly blend. Work it with sandals, boots, heels, flats, tights, or bare legs.

## 9. BALLET FLATS

Whether you choose stretch-back "scrunchie" flats, structured flats with a small half-inch heel, or slipper flats, these make every girl feel feminine. In every imaginable color, fabric, and embellishment, flats provide comfort with style and give your feet a break.

**BEST CHOICE** A structured, tapered toe flat with a firm sole is class but comfy and won't look like slippers.

## 10. A SOFT, OVERSIZE SCARF

A large, lightweight scarf draped at the neck adds color, texture, personality, and style to anything from suits to dresses or jeans. Look for those with newsy prints (depending on trends, this can be anything from batik to techno prints), hints of sequins or shimmer, trims of sparkly stones, or fringe. A scarf always adds a cool touch. Gives a dress or suit a whole new style and looks great with jeans.

**BEST CHOICE** A lightweight printed scarf in a matte or gauzy fabric that drapes well and won't slip, in a face-flattering color with a touch of sparkle from metallic threads, crystals, or a splatter of sequins.

# SUPER-SUCCESSFUL WOMEN CEOS

As you know, women can be high achievers at any age and still have plenty of style. Certain fashion items work for everyone and have the ability to transform quickly. Some, like pencil skirts, ballet flats, and a crisp, striped shirt, may already be in your closet. Others may be new to you, but my Gretta-guarantee makes every item on this list a must-have.

**The Weekend Girls look polished head-to-toe with an accessible attitude.**

LAUREN BUSH, 26, cofounder of FEED, a non-profit that provides fifty million meals worldwide

KERRY KNEE, 42, CEO of Flirty Girl Fitness, thought up pole dancing and belly dancing as a workout

DYLAN LAUREN, 38, CEO of Dylan's Candy Bar, largest candy store in the world

KATRINA MARKOFF, 39, CEO of Vosges Chocolates

STACY SNIDER, 51, CEO and cochairman of DreamWorks Studios

**The Girly Girls have a flair for the feminine and a brain for business.**

SOFIA AMORUSO, 26, cofounder and CEO of Nasty Gal, a site selling new and vintage clothing

TORY BURCH, 46, CEO of her eponymous brand

DANIELLE SNYDER and JODIE SNYDER, 25 and 28, founders of jewelry company Dannijo

OPRAH WINFREY, 59, CEO of OWN

**The Sophisticated Girls are cool, classy, and nothing intimidates them.**

ALEXA VON TOBEL, 26, CEO of LearnVest.com, a site focused on helping women develop good financial habits early in life.

MARISSA MAYER, 37, CEO of Yahoo!

ELLEN J. KULLMAN, 56, CEO of DuPont

ARIANNA HUFFINGTON, 62, chair, president, and editor-in-chief of the Huffington Post Media Group

INDRA NOOYI, 57, CEO of PepsiCo

**The Sexy Girls enjoy their diva status but don't let it get in the way of the deal.**

JENNIFER HYMAN, 31, cofounder of Rent the Runway, which lets you rent dresses and accessories from more than 100 designers and brands

MINDY GROSSMAN, 55, CEO of HSN

NATALIE MASSENET, 46, CEO of Net-a-Porter

DESIRÉE ROGERS, 57, CEO of Johnson Publishing Company, which publishes *Ebony* and *Jet* magazines

# THE OMG! MOMENT

OF COURSE, SOMEONE IS ALWAYS GOING TO BE LOOKING AT YOU AND WONDERING HOW OLD YOU ARE. NEVER MIND THAT. DON'T LET YOUR REAL AGE LIMIT YOU. YOUR STYLE, NOT YOUR AGE, USUALLY IS THE DEAL-BREAKER. AS A BUYER FOR MY STORES AND A STYLIST, I'M ALWAYS THINKING ABOUT HOW TO STRETCH THE BOUNDARIES OF NEW TRENDS SO THEY CAN BE MORE WEARABLE FOR A DIVERSE GROUP OF GIRLS WITH VERY DIFFERENT BODIES, LIFESTYLES, AND STYLE BLUEPRINTS. THERE ARE INSIDER TIPS TO LEARN.

Since every new designer trend filters down to stores and low-cost brands on a scale of trendiness from subtle to extreme, you have a lot of options. Adding understated, trendy touches of color, texture, pattern, and accessories is easy for anyone to do. But as a stylist, I know varying the flavor of your basic style recipe with just a few ingredients can quickly change the entire taste of the meal.

When you're putting together new looks each season and integrating trends into your established style, be strategic. Here are examples of how to manipulate your iconic style up and down to successfully create the "age attitude" you want. Let's use a work dress as the base look.

## Gretta-quette

Here I am in 1998 at the opening of my first grettacole luxury spa/salon/boutique in Boston, Massachusetts. I am wearing a consignment splurge for the occasion— a Giorgio Armani fur-collar tailored suit that fit the fancy evening cocktail bash. This was my first taste of being a CEO.

At the opening of my boutique with my friend Nicole, 1998.

# THE **Weekend Girl**
## WEARING A SHIRTDRESS

Choose belted shirtdresses with a fit and flare shape. Super-casual loose styles that resemble night shirts are not what we're after.

**DIALS UP POLISH AND EXPERIENCE BY ADDING:**

Low heels
+ a trench or long, belted cardigan

A leather belt
+ cage shoes or shoe-booties
+ statement bag

**DIALS DOWN TO A YOUTHFUL, EDGIER LOOK BY ADDING:**

A jean jacket
+ strappy sandals

A hip belt
+ espadrilles or gladiator sandals

# THE **Girly Girl**
## WEARING AN A-LINE DRESS

Nothing is easier to wear than an A-line dress no matter what your shape. Shoulder to waist is fitted and then flares to a feminine finish at the knee.

**DIALS UP EXPERIENCE AND POLISH BY ADDING:**

A cropped jacket
+ an embellished belt
+ feminine pumps

A tailored, matching coat
+ a ladylike bag in a bold color

**DIALS DOWN TO A YOUTHFUL, EDGIER LOOK BY ADDING:**

A pop-of-color cardigan
+ cage booties

A T-shirt under the dress
+ jeweled strappy sandals

# THE **Sophisticated Girl**
## WEARING A SHEATH

A sheath shows your shape, so keep it tailored, streamlined, and business-like with the right neck and hem.

**DIALS UP EXPERIENCE AND POLISH BY ADDING:**

Lace-up oxfords
+ an oversized satchel
+ big, dark sunglasses

A blazer
+ high-heel pumps
+ an exotic bag

**DIALS DOWN TO A YOUTHFUL, EDGIER LOOK BY ADDING:**

A sweater knotted over her shoulders
+ sunglasses as a headband
+ slipper flats

A cardigan belted over the dress
+ structured ballet flats

# THE Sexy Girl
## WEARING A JERSEY DRESS

Choose a full-coverage wrap that won't disclose too much cleavage or thigh. These are ideal travelers for heavy commuting or business travel since they don't crease or wrinkle.

**DIALS UP EXPERIENCE AND POLISH BY ADDING:**

Platform pumps
+ a cropped leather jacket

A print blazer
+ chain-link bracelets

**DIALS DOWN TO A YOUTHFUL, EDGIER LOOK BY ADDING:**

A leather biker jacket
+ cuff stilettos

Fringed boots or booties
+ neon tights

# TRENDING UP: HOW FAR TO GO AND STILL LOOK LIKE YOU

NOT EVERY TREND WILL BE LOVE AT FIRST SIGHT. IN FACT, NOW THAT YOU KNOW YOUR STYLE, SOME TRENDS ARE CLEAR CASES OF "NOT FOR ME!" FIGURE OUT WHERE ON THE TREND-O-METER YOUR STYLE AND AGE MESH SEAMLESSLY. WHETHER YOU'RE TWENTY-TWO, THIRTY-TWO, OR FORTY-TWO, YOU CAN PULL OFF ANY LOOK ON YOUR INSPIRATION BOARD AND KEEP UPDATING YOUR STYLE AS TRENDS DEVELOP.

First you need to decide how far out to go without losing credibility. You never want to miss an opportunity because you're young and dressing too old or are old and dressing too young. Finding the right balance for you each season is essential.

Designers play with fit, proportion, fabrics, and color to make news and sell clothes. It's up to you to check new trends against your blueprint for style (this is where that constantly evolving checklist comes in handy again!) and figure out how to adapt them into your look. I know certain trends are tricky to navigate, and designers change what's hot every season, which only adds to the confusion. So let's clear up any misconceptions about age and style. Not every new trend will work for every girl, but that has to do with your body, lifestyle, and personal style more than it has to do with age. The key is to never let clothes date you. Here's how to ignore age, refresh your wardrobe, and stay consistent when fashion keeps changing its mind.

# GRETTA'S AGE-FREE STYLE DANGER-DODGERS

### Mis-match.

Never opt for a prepackaged look where everything "works together" as the designer or store shows it. Matchy-matchy at any age shows a lack of personality and individuality and looks "old" in attitude. When I go to the shows or showrooms to check out what's new, I'm constantly breaking down the looks (mentally or physically) and moving the pieces around in different ways. Even when you buy a suit, take the top and bottom apart and try them with different tops, skirts, pants, sweaters, and jeans in the dressing room. Get adventurous about mixing fabrics and clothes you wouldn't usually wear together. Shiny dressy pieces can work mixed with matte ones for day—for example, a metallic tank under a tweed jacket or a sequin skirt with a pebble-knit sweater and booties. Mixing feminine dresses, blouses, and skirts with tougher, edgier shoes and boots or leather pieces can work whether you're a Weekend, Girly, Sophisticated, or Sexy Girl.

### Be your own brand.

No head-to-toe looks! Never wear a curated look from one store or brand top to bottom. The window display in J. Crew or Eileen Fisher may look great on the mannequin, but this is how fashion victims get suckered into looks that aren't really them.

Buy items, not looks. Then go back to your closet and give that new item your own personal twist. Mixing classic and trendy, pricey and low-cost with ease is the sign you've become a fashion pro. Flirt with new brands, and try new labels, too—there's no reason to stay faithful. You just might discover better sources that suit your budget and style. The things to avoid for those with womanly shapes are stores and brands that use junior-fit models for sizing. The proportions, waist, rise, and length rarely work out although the prices and displays seem appealing.

### Get fit.

Being lazy about the way clothes fit can age you in either direction in a bad way. Take new items to the tailor to customize them and bring in old ones for an update. Anything that's really off the charts fit-wise—too big, too bare, too short, too tight, too long—has got to go. Yes, this will increase your closet maintenance, but it's worth the results. Two tired and tacky proportions no one ever needs to bother trying—a wide, boxy top with wide-leg pants, and a skimpy, bare top with a tight mini.

### Keep it fresh.

Don't let history repeat itself. If you wore a trend once before, it's never the same this time around.

Proportions, details, and the way the trend is put together always change. For example, if full skirts are back, check the length, the shoe, and the top. Is it being worn with a bootie and a body-hugging top, or with a tee, cropped jacket, and flats? Does the skirt work for your current look and body? There is no such thing as age appropriate; there's simply attitude appropriate. Keep your vintage/retro pieces, but mix them with new pieces too.

### Keep retro pieces as accents.

You never want to look vintage even if you buy clothes from a consignment shop. We all love icons like Jackie O, Audrey Hepburn, and Marilyn Monroe, but you don't want to replicate their look today in an identical way.

### Let fancy pieces work.

Avoid overloading already-busy printed dresses and decorative jackets, embellished tops, and patterned pants or skirts with too many distracting extras, especially lots of jewelry. It makes you look overdone and lacking focus. Make a strong statement, not three strong statements. When in doubt, keep it simple—a shoe, bag, and belt may be all you really need.

# EDIT TRENDS FOR YOU

When a new trend appeals, decide where it fits in your bigger overall scheme. Let's take a trend like retro-inspired peplums for example.

While a cherry red or bright pink peplum dress might flounce its way easily into the Girly Girl's style, maybe a zip-front peplum jacket would give the Sophisticated Girl a fresh alternative to pair with pencil skirts and slim pants. The Weekend Girl might opt for a sleeveless, stretch-knit peplum top for jeans, while the Sexy Girl might choose a faux leather peplum top to wear with skinnies and booties. You control which trends to add and how much trendiness you want.

What dates some girls' closets is clinging to a look too tightly. They're afraid to try something new. This is why I keep emphasizing the importance of updating your inspiration board and checklist as you go. Others jump on every trend

## Gretta's Rule of FIVE

When the media hype of runway news and stores packed with new merchandise seems overwhelming, five items always pull the Successful Girl through a trend frenzy. If you buy nothing else, you can't go wrong with these five foolproof rejuvenators:

**A SHOE-OF-THE-MINUTE** It may be a platform, strappy cage, shoe-bootie, gladiator boot, a black patent pump, or a metallic peep-toe, but wearing the hot shoe carries you through the season.

**A LARGER-THAN-LIFE COCKTAIL RING CONVERSA-TION STARTER** This is pointer power! A major statement ring nets big style from a small change.

**A QUILTED LEATHER BAG** Guaranteed chic, from the iconic chain-strap shoulder bag to ladylike satchels and structured bags, quilting looks rich.

without considering whether it works for them, or buy into it too deeply before making a test run with one piece. The degree of trendiness you opt to select has an impact on how your style-age is perceived. Evaluate trends and decide what level of involvement you want. No Successful Girl wants to look like a fashion victim or as if the clothes are wearing her.

## A POWER POLISH

The devil may wear Prada, but diva digits are a successful style detail that cannot be overlooked. Stay away from a predictable colors such as basic pink or red. You don't need tricky, complicated nail art, just one amazing "of the moment" luxe lacquer.

## A WHITE OR BRIGHT COAT

It may be a bathrobe wrap, swingy trapeze, voluminous cocoon, or button-up, tailored topcoat, but that unexpected flash of color brings everything under it to life.

## Here's where it works and where it doesn't.

### THE GIRL WHO KNOWS TOO MUCH

trends things up so much that she loses any sense of what her personal style is. She lacks restraint and shows poor judgment by choosing the most extreme looks as she hits every trend-of-the-season in an effort to appear younger or cooler. She may be wearing waxed emerald-green jeans with metallic silver oxfords, a patchwork satchel that's a mash-up of colorful exotic skins, a lace top with opaque side panels, under a leather-sleeved blazer, with nails covered in a rainbow of blue glitter, double false lashes, and a dark red matte lipstick.

### THE GIRL WHO KNOWS TOO LITTLE

thinks she looks too young and inexperienced and tries to compensate with clothes that make her appear older. Instead, they work in the other direction. She may be wearing a matched suit with a plain knit shell, low round-toe pumps, a dainty necklace and studs that don't register as jewelry, and a leather shoulder bag she bought years ago and never used. She looks ageless but agelessly old.

### THE SUCCESSFUL GIRL

gets it right! She balances trends and wardrobe staples for an update that's consistent with her style and right for any age. She may be wearing a black leather pencil, a multicolor floral silk peplum blouse, oxblood peep-toe booties, and carrying an embossed leather satchel.

# THE GRETTA STYLE-OVER

JUDY HADN'T GIVEN HER STYLE A THOUGHT FOR DECADES, BUT SHE'S REALLY A SEXY GIRL UNDERNEATH ALL THOSE SHAPELESS LAYERS. THE MINUTE I PUT HER IN LEOPARD AND RECHARGED HER HAIR AND MAKEUP, THE YEARS DISSOLVED. SHE FOUND HER PERFECT RECIPE FOR LOOKING AGELESS AND REDISCOVERED HER BODY.

after

before

# CHAPTER 6

# BODY CONFI- DENCE AND SUCCESS

YOU'VE GOT THE BASICS DOWN, and you understand your style and how to work your wardrobe in a strategic way. Now it's time to take things up a notch. Think of it as style graduate school. I believe in style at any size and in celebrating your shape. The Successful Girl always wants to put her best body forward, and the clothes you choose can do that. We're all hung up on body issues and often in denial about how much to conceal and reveal. I find the biggest mistake women make is to overdress their flaws and hide in loose, shapeless clothes. Their wardrobe becomes a crutch and does them a disservice. This chapter is all about working with your silhouette and style to achieve a successful look.

As a stylist and fashion pro, the first thing I do with a new client or a makeover candidate is ask her to disrobe. I need to see your true shape. On the *Rachael Ray Show*, makeovers often come in from out of town, and we meet in person on set. I always ask for preliminary photos taken in a swimsuit, undies, shorts, and tank—as little as possible—first before the segment. This gives me a more accurate read than relying on size, measurements, and weight.

The Successful Girl must audit and edit her undies— anything frayed, worn out, faded; or too embarassing for anyone to see should be tossed.

The Successful Girl takes control of her shape without giving up her style. You can too. All you need is an attitude adjustment.

*The Successful Girl takes control of her shape without giving up her style. You can too. All you need is an attitude adjustment.*

# THE GOTTA-HAVES

**This is your body confidence kit**

You always want your clothes—whether you're a Weekend, Girly, Sophisticated or Sexy Girl—to look their best. This may mean giving your usual bra and panties an upgrade in control to make your silhouette 100% successful. There are ten items I rely on to balance and improve every body from size two to sixteen and on into the plus-size range. These hardworking foundation pieces compress, lift, and smooth your shape for a firmer, bulge-free look. Be sure to buy shapewear pieces in the right size. Shapers that are a size too small can emphasize or create bulges with too much compression or ride up at the bottom. You don't want to feel squeezed, just sleek.

## 1. A TUMMY-SMOOTHING HIGH-WAIST BRIEF

Hide bloating, post-vacation or after-holiday tummy bulge (let's be honest; we all indulge on occasion) with this item that flattens and holds you in.

**BEST CHOICE** A black or nude brief with a maximum control panel in front. Try a thong back style for no panty line

## 2. A BIKER-SHORT BODYSUIT

This one-piece shaper is like a swimsuit with mid-thigh legs. It smooths everything chest-down in one swoop and gives you a toned look under separate tops and bottoms or dresses. Some styles are scooped to provide space for your choice of bra. Other styles have built-in shelf bras or constructed cups and underwire to make wearing a bra unnecessary. The latter work best for small to medium chests. Stick to black when wearing a short skirt or dress. There's nothing worse than catching a glimpse of nude shapewear as you get into/out of a car.

**BEST CHOICE** A firm, control style in nude or black that allows you to wear your own bra.

## 3. A CONTROL CAPRI BODYSUIT

Longer than the biker-short bodysuit in #2, this shaper extends to mid-calf or ankle length. It gives heavy legs a sleek look under jeans, fitted pants, pantsuits, tuxedo suits, and long evening or bridal gowns.

**BEST CHOICE**
Seamless black or nude.

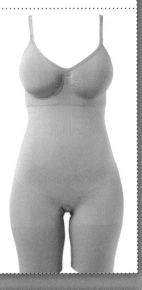

## 4. A MOLDED STRAPLESS BRA

This bra has a contoured pre-fabricated shape to build up small or saggy chests. It gives a shapelier, more lifted look (especially from the side), adds fullness and volume, and hoists your girls to the right level.

**BEST CHOICE** A foam-filled contour bra with optional or convertible straps in black or nude.

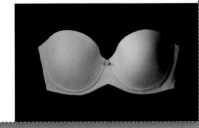

## 7. A BUTT-BOOSTING SHAPER

These work like a push-up bra for your derriere in a brief- or biker-length short. Having a well-rounded booty has never been more in fashion, and the strategic compression in the back lifts and shapes.

**BEST CHOICE** Nude or black in the leg length that works for you (girls with thigh issues will feel best in the longer, mid-thigh length).

## 8. A CONTROL SLIP

Look smoother in skirts and dresses with a half-or full-style slip. They look feminine enough to be date-worthy in smooth (frill-free) or lacy embellished styles. Some full-length shaper slips styles have built-in bras; others work with your own bra.

**BEST CHOICE** A full-length smooth shaper slip in black and nude you can wear with your own bras.

## 5. A FULL-COVERAGE T-SHIRT BRA

This is the perfect everyday bra under tees, thin knits, blouses, and lightweight dresses. Made of a very light foam fill, it prevents nipple show-though and prevents sag. Because the design totally covers your breast front and side, there's no cleavage compression or pit bulge to worry about.

**BEST CHOICE** A black or nude, full-coverage, opaque, seamless, smooth, contour bra.

## 6. SEAMLESS MICROFIBER PANTIES

High-leg panties in a silky microfiber fabric disappear under clothes when you're not wearing a panty-style shaper. Match them to your bra. (This is the only time I suggest matching anything, but when it comes to undies, it does look better.) They're available in high or low waist, thong-back or full-coverage rear.

**BEST CHOICE** Black and nude (to work with all your bras), high waist, thong back.

## 9. BLACK CONTROL LEGGINGS

These are thicker and more opaque than everyday stretch-cotton leggings and have increased compression to firm jiggles. The reinforced fabric and tummy control panel holds you in and won't sag, bag, or thin out after repeated washings.

**BEST CHOICE** Dense matte black with extra compression at the tummy.

## 10. A CONTOUR CAMISOLE

This is a low-dose control tank that comes in simple, unadorned and feminine, lacy styles. It uses stretch plus subtle compression to stabilize your bust (less bounce) and provide a smooth, seamless line from bra to hips. Wear it under light sweaters, knits, and blouses.

**BEST CHOICE** A nude or black frill-free style that works over your bras.

# GRETTA'S GRIPES

To dress successfully, you need to acknowledge and work with your real body . . . not the body you want, the one you really have. In my work as a stylist, I've identified ten key issues that prevent women from feeling and dressing their best. Sometimes these concerns are valid since they affect the way clothes fit, but often they unfortunately encourage women to overcompensate for perceived flaws in shapeless, loose clothes. Successful Girls know a mind-shift can turn perceived flaws into assets. When girls focus on:

## Being Too Tall

They've been standing, walking, and sitting hunched over since their teens. They feel clothes are too short or their long arms and torso appear mannish. The truth is, tall girls have the ideal (and very coveted) height of a top fashion model. Taylor Swift, Uma Thurman, Nicole Kidman, Kimora Lee, Maria Sharapova, and Aisha Tyler top 5'10" or more. Work on having fantastic posture.

## Being Too Short

They have what I call "small petite syndrome." They complain about feeling too cute, childlike, or "stumpy"—like they're wearing their mother's clothes. They think "petite" lines are frumpy and limiting, and major alterations are just part of life. They want to look sexy and sophisticated. The key is to not continue to

make height an obstacle. Small women who project a confident, self-assured attitude can wear whatever they like. Reese Witherspoon, Kim Kardashian, Jennifer Love Hewitt, Jada Pinkett Smith, and Kristen Chenoweth are all 5'2" or less.

## A Heavy Chest

They feel too busty and dress totally around their chest. They say button front blouses and shirts always gape. If they go up a size to compensate for their chest, the fit elsewhere is too big (at the shoulder, waist, and arms, for example). They hide in loose, big tops. The right bra in the right size is crucial to fashion success (see my fit tips later on in this chapter). FYI, the average bra size is now 36C, and implant procedures are trending up, so turn this into a positive. Look at Katy Perry, Sofia

Vergara, Salma Hayek, Christina Hendricks, Jessica Simpson, and Brooklyn Decker!

## A Flat Chest

They wear padded bras 24/7 to compensate and dress around their small chest with layers of clothes to add volume. They worry about being too small on top and being disproportionately bigger below the waist, and they often are—that's the real issue that needs to be addressed. (See my body silhouette strategy further on in this chapter.) Celebs like Claire Danes and Kate Winslet have that issue too. However, if you're all-over slim with a flat chest like Keira Knightley , Kate Hudson, or Cameron Diaz, for example, dressing to flatter is fairly simple since you're not dressing around a big bust.

## A Big Butt

They always want to minimize the rear even though it's now a major asset—look at J.Lo and Kim Kardashian! Getting the right jeans (and pants and skirts) is the major concern. If jeans fit at the butt, the waist is too big and gapes or the legs are too wide. Learning how to select the right cuts for you on sight is essential.

## A Flat Butt

They always feel they have a droopy bottom or a diaper look and never feel sexy in fitted clothes. They compensate by looking for dresses and skirts with volume like A-lines and shapers that lift and amplify the booty. Pippa Middleton's small derriere made headlines all over the world, but she clearly knows how to flaunt it.

## Heavy Legs

They worry about thunder thighs in jeans and even pencil skirts, and sleek, fitted dresses cause concerns. If the fit at the thighs is OK, it may not be at the waist and hips. They feel too many trendy shoes and boots are so appealing but emphasize chunky calves and ankles. Strong, muscular, fit legs are now sexy as Jessica Simpson, Beyoncé, Scarlett Johansson, and Vanessa Hudgens have proven and played up in sexy high heels and booties.

## Chicken Legs

They never want to show their legs and hide out in wide-leg pants and boyfriend jeans. They have model-slim legs but don't know how to make them work to their advantage. Miley Cyrus, Alexa Chung, and Victoria Beckham have slim legs and wear skirts, shorts, and anything else they want, including the most attention-getting heels that draw attention to their legs!

## Heavy Arms

They feel weight gain shows in their arms and are embarrassed by soft, untoned, chubby upper arms. Nearly 95% of clients and makeover candidates lift their arms and show me how the excess dangles and waves. They wear heavy, thick knits and jackets in an attempt to cover them. Every woman from Queen Latifah to Jennifer Lawrence has a little extra underarm—look at all the celebs walking the red carpet in strapless gowns! However, since First Lady Michelle Obama has made buff arms a major fashion goal, toning up arms is on every girl's agenda. It also is one of the fastest, easiest things to do if you work out with mini weights at home.

## Skinny Arms

They don't recognize an asset when they have it and rarely show their arms. Usually, these arms are very beautiful and just need the right armhole or a subtle sleeve like a cap or elbow length. Heidi Klum, Angelina Jolie, and Sarah Jessica Parker have ballerina-slim arms and show them to advantage.

*Successful Girls know a mind-shift can turn perceived flaws into assets.*

# SECRETS OF SHAPE SUCCESS

Every woman (even celebs and models) has one or more of these ten so-called body problems to deal with. In fact, our bodies are usually a compilation of issues. Some change as we work out, change our lifestyles, and lose or gain weight, but most concerns stick with us. You can be tall and chesty or short with skinny arms and heavy legs for example. You can tone up or lose weight, but your basic body shape always stays the same.

My philosophy is different from other body-type/style-strategies you may have read about. I believe the secret of successful dressing is to identify your overall body silhouette—the outline of your body. Forget for now your dress,

jeans, or bra size. The shape of the outline of your body is what counts. Every girl's body falls into one of three silhouettes: straight up and down, bottom heavy, or top heavy. Don't get side-tracked by body features, size, weight, or skin tone. Once you identify your silhouette, my shape for success system simplifies every other issue with your best body fit. This lesson takes your style—Girly or Sexy, Weekend or Sophisticated—to the next level. You may at this point even be blurring the boundaries a little as you gain experience and skill working with your style. For example, a Girly Girl might be adding a black leather jacket to her look, but it may have a peplum or a ruffle trim. A Sophisticated Girl might be buying a new tailored suit, but it may have an asymmetric jacket and a pencil skirt with leather side panels. Before we start, one last thing to remember: None of these three silhouettes is better to have than the others, so keep reading. You only have more style to gain!

## Gretta-quette

My own silhouette is bottom heavy although that never stops my style. This fit-and-flare red dress follows my strategy with an upper body enhancing neckline and A-line skirt.

# THE OMG! MOMENT

So, silhouette counts more than being an XS or L, a 4 or a 14, 105 pounds or 150. Identifying your body silhouette accurately, once and for all, makes looking great easier and more accessible for any girl.

To illustrate this concept take a look at my GRETTA SHAPE GUIDES. Each one is designed to reveal how a Successful Girl of any size fits into one of the three overall silhouettes.

Study these illustrations and you'll understand why and how so many women of different sizes can wear the same clothes and have a similar successful style. The only difference comes with height, since the taller you, are the more body space you have to work with, and height influences proportions. Now let me show you how use this info to improve the way your clothes fit and perform. Read through each of the three body silhouettes to find the one that matches your own. This will help you refine the items you wear for maximum flattery.

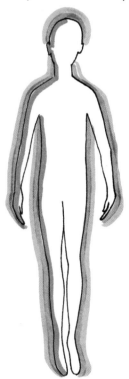

Keira Knightly
Clare Danes
Cameron Diaz

*The straight up + down*

Shoulders and hips nearly the same width with no defined waist

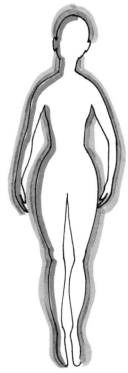

Jennifer Love Hewitt
Beyonce
Kim Kardashian

*The bottom-heavy*

Width of your shoulders and torso are smaller than the width of your hips

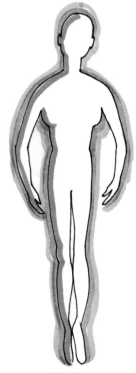

Katy Perry
Salma Hayek
Queen Latifah

*The top-heavy*

Width of shoulders and boobs wider than hips

# THE STRAIGHT UP + DOWN SILHOUETTE

When you stand naked in front of a full-length mirror, your shoulders and hips are equal, and there is little or no body definition between. You may be skinny, saggy, athletic, or a bit chunky. Your shape is sometimes referred to as a boy shape or androgynous. Designers use fit models to drape and shape clothing samples, and they usually have this kind of curve-free body. The secret to this silhouette is to use your clothes to build curves. Don't confuse adding curves with adding bulk, though. You want to create more body definition, the illusion of a waist, and/or a voluptuous S-shape. Taylor Swift, Keira Knightly, and Kelly Bensimone are examples of straight up and down silhouettes that get it right. Here are the items that do this for you:

## Tops

Start with your favorite curve-building necklines. Make scoops, wraps, Vs, draped, cowl, and sweetheart shapes first choices. Stick with body-hugging tees, sweaters, and shirts in stretch blends with draping, ruching, or details like ruffles or bows down the front or sides that add to the curve-boosting. Slip into a molded or slightly padded bra or even a shaper bodysuit to ramp up your body and confidence. Soft, feminine blouses with decorative fronts or peplums also fake a shapelier look. Wrap tops in jersey or cotton knit and crisp stretch-cotton shirts transform straight shapes into sensuous Vs and give your waist instant definition. Here's how it works for our style blueprint: A Sophisticated Girl might do a crisp, white cotton, wrap shirt; the Weekend Girl might do a V sweater; the Girly Girl might opt for a ruffled blouse; and the Sexy Girl might choose a scoop-neck top. Choose T-back and asymmetric one-shoulder tops or draped halters to carve out sexy shoulders. Any blouse or top with a satiny sheen, sequins, shimmer, or shine reflects light to maximize shape. Satin and sequins work in your favor. So do small all-over swirly prints like florals, abstract graphics, and animal prints.

## Skirts

A leg-revealing pencil skirt that hits mid thigh, above the knees, or to the top of knees emphasizes shapeliness. Those with draping, peplums, a flare at the hem (sometimes called a trumpet pencil), or slight tucking below the waist for subtle volume (sometimes called a tulip pencil), and knit pencils are effective. A-line, pleated, tiered, and flared skirts break up the straight up and down silhouette and suggest curves too.

## Dresses

Your best curve-curating dresses include belted shirtdresses, shapely sheaths (tailored or knit), belted

**Bicolor dresses break up the body with sections of color and suggest a shapelier you.**

**Define your waist when-ever possible with belts, color, texture, and fabric breaks between tops and bottoms. Any time you don't, you risk looking bigger, straighter, and more shapeless.**

sheaths and A-lines, fit-and-flare styles with a defined waist, wrap dresses, ruched or draped stretch jerseys, and dresses cut on the bias. Look for body-clinging sweaterdresses and ruched jersey dresses that turn your curves into an S-shape. Bicolor dresses (called colorblock, too) break up the body with sections of color—top and bottom or in side panels—and suggest a shapelier you.

## Pants + jeans

You're going to benefit most from narrow, slim, ankle-cropped or cigarette styles, leggings, skinny or fitted straight-leg jeans with stretch, and straight-leg trousers. Pants are not tricky for this silhouette.

## Jackets

Beef up curves with contoured jackets that are nipped in at the waist. They can be tailored that way, belted or a wrap style, or shaped by a peplum. Cropped trenches are always a win, so are cropped fitted jackets, asymmetric jackets that close off-center instead of straight down the front suggest sensuous swerves and can be anything from a biker to a clean-lined minimalist style.

## Coats

Look for interpretations of the jackets above, especially wrap or belted styles. Trenches are perfect for this body silhouette and so are fit-and-flare styles (sometimes known as princess style). For taller straight-up-and-down bodies, double-breasted coats and pea coats work since the height makes up for double-layered fabric and buttons.

# THE BOTTOM-HEAVY SILHOUETTE

When you stand naked in front of your full-length mirror, your hips and/or thighs are the attention getters. Your body from the waist down is disproportionately wider, fuller, and more generous than your top half. You may also have a tummy or a bountiful booty to add to the body equation, but that's covered by our gotta-haves and these silhouette solutions, so relax. This is a very common body shape, and you have two choices. Embrace it and wear fitted tops and full or A-line skirts with statement belts to highlight your slim waist. The other option is to use your clothes strategically to create a more balanced look. For example, bring more attention to your upper body with a bright blazer or embellished cardigan. You're in charge of your style, but the more disproportionate your body, the fewer choices you have to bridge the gap. Some women in the public eye appear to be curvy and balanced. In truth, they're bottom-heavy silhouettes and just cleverly manipulate their clothes to say otherwise. Kim Kardashian (Sexy), Michelle Obama (Girly), and Beyoncé (Sexy) are actually bottom-heavy girls who manage their styles and shapes well. Here are your best selections:

## Tops

You're amazing in statement tops with embellished necklines or bow blouses, brilliant colors, shimmery fabrics, bold prints, or horizontal stripes. Any neckline that optically creates width is a hip/thigh balancer. Wide Vs, scoops, boat-necks, off-shoulder cuts, and draped necklines do that effortlessly. Sleeves that slightly extend the shoulder line, like cap sleeves and puffs, create a stronger shoulder line. For summer and evenings, one-shoulder and off-shoulder tops get attention going above the waist or go strapless with a statement necklace.

## Skirts

A-line skirts are your staple, but straight, slim pencils work well in sturdy fabrics like leather, textured cotton, wool stretch blends in flat or textured lace, velvet, denim, or brocade. Look for back- or side-zip styles with no waistband or a narrow one that sits at or just below your natural waist. Slightly relaxed pencils with draping, a wrap, or flared trumpet style that flips out at the hem flatter bottom-heavy silhouettes with muscular or full-figure thighs. Tiered pencils and slim pleated skirts in soft, light fabrics like chiffon or silk provides camouflage and shape.

## Dresses

If your arms rock, you're the perfect candidate for a sleeveless dress. Don't hesitate to throw on an eye-catching belt either. A-shape sheaths and fit-and-flare styles provide base looks with an enormous range of color, print, and fabric options for day or evening. They also work well with a cropped jacket for a suit look

or a decorative cardigan for a contemporary twist. A wrap dress in an all-over small print is a quick solution for bottom-heavy girls. The V wrap creates a reverse triangle shape on top that balances

width below, while the self-tie waist highlights and amplifies a trim waist. Embellished and draped necklines and wide scoops or Vs attract the eye up and put extra emphasis above the waist for balance. Color-blocked dresses with darker hues below the waist or at the sides for a panel effect are all flattering looks for bottom-heavy shapes.

Every girl wants sexy statement shoes and booties whether her legs are chunky or slim. Feeling great in your power shoes is all that counts.

## Pants + jeans

Spend more time on these pieces than anything else in your closet for a precise fit that flatters hips, rear, and thighs. Medium-rise, fitted, straight-leg jeans or fitted medium-rise skinnies in a dark rinse can provide a slim base for your more eye-catching tops, which can be anything from a trimmed tunic to a shaped blazer. Slim or straight pants in a stretch blend keep your bottom half sleek. Choose simple, unadorned styles with angled pockets or none at all. Pantsuits with a crisp jacket and lean, tailored line give a uniform look head-to-toe—just keep the jacket details consistent with those listed below.

## Jackets

Your jackets can be standouts and attract attention and/or just add a more balanced look to the body because they have some degree of structure (and even knit jackets do). You have lots of choices: a wrapped, contoured, or belted jacket; a cropped, fitted jacket; an A-line jacket with three-quarter sleeves; or a contrast-trim blazer. The newest jackets have very discreet padding at the shoulder that builds up the line without an obvious extended or fake look. Skip boxy, boyfriend styles that hide your figure.

## Coats

A straight, slim, man-tailored, single-breasted coat, trench (and this refers not just to raincoats but any coat cut in this style), and A-line, princess or fit-and-flare styles flatter you. These super-classic shapes look chic with everything and even out any imbalances in proportion.

# THE TOP-HEAVY SILHOUETTE

When you stand naked in front of a full-length mirror, your body waist-up is wider, fuller, and more attention-getting and slimmer waist down. You may have broad swimmer's shoulders or a large chest and soft, full upper arms that enhance that proportion. When you gain weight, it goes straight to your boobs and arms. Your silhouette is the opposite of bottom heavy. Most women opt for creating a more balanced silhouette in this case. It opens up more options for you, but again, the more disproportionate you are, the more fixed your strategy.

## Tops

If you're very busty, be sure to start with a major support bra collection. The biggest mistake top-heavy women make is wearing the wrong size bra. A new bra should fit on the last set of hooks to the point where you almost think it's too tight. Busty girls always choose a bigger band size when they really need a smaller band and a bigger cup size. For example, a girl might wear a 36C when what she really needs is a 34D. Your bra band is too loose if you can fit a finger easily beneath or it moves around. The band has to be very snug since this is where your bras stretch over time. Wear a bra band that's the right width to support and cover your chest and avoid back bulges. If you have a wider back, a wider bra band is a must, and beautiful bras with wider bands are easy to find. Put on your best bra and stand sideways in the mirror. The fullest part of your bust should be (on an imaginary line encircling your body) right below your armpit, not any lower. Full breasts when not properly supported make you look fuller and fatter. Learning how to manage your breasts for success is part of this body silhouette's solution.

Top-heavy silhouettes benefit most from open necklines that reveal the neck and upper chest, like wide shallow Vs and scoops, draped necklines, and any button-front shirt, blouse, or top that unbuttons to a mid-chest V. They elongate your neck and entire torso. Wraps are important to this silhouette since you can adjust the fit and define your waist. Stick to opaque, light knits in tees and sweaters—no cables, ribs, or bells and whistles. You want to take the focus away from your boobs and yet acknowledge them in a positive way. A fitted peplum top with a slash or V-neck can stretch your torso and balance upper body with waist definition and curves at the hip. Wear it over a narrow pant, skinny jean, or pencil skirt. For casual moments, slim, slouchy, lightweight sweaters and tunics over fitted jeans are a great laid-back look.

## Skirts

With your slimmer bottom half, you're a prime candidate for a "wow" statement skirt. You can wear almost any A-line or pencil, but those that pull attention away from your top half with texture, print or color will help create a more balanced silhouette. Just avoid the deadly combo of big chest, tight mini, and heels (or trendy short-shorts, heels, and a big chest). Do pumps, platforms, booties, cage booties, shoe booties, gladiator boots, strappy sandals, and clingy, stretch, knee-high boots with a skirt that has some volume and movement.

## Dresses

Dresses with volume below the waist, sleek, crisp lines, or wrap styles balance the top-heavy silhouette. An A-line sheath or shift, fit-and-flare style, or a slim-straight shift in tailored and knit versions can't miss—neither can a two-tone dress that's darker on top and lighter or brighter below the waist. Adjustable jersey wrap dresses create a flattering V, define the waist, give extra support to your boobs, and have a feminine flash of leg and a flippy attitude at the hem that's irresistible. All-over prints for tailored or wrap styles unify the body since they work like camouflage to fool the eye and keep it moving. You can't zero in on bulges easily.

## Pants + jeans

Lucky you can wear statement pants and jeans too. The thinking is identical to skirts. Keep the shape below the waist narrow with leggings, skinnies, fitted jeans, ankle-cropped pants, or straight tailored pants. But you get to focus attention on your bottom with more color, print, and texture.

## Jackets

Adding a top layer to tees, tanks, blouses, and shirts has to be very planned. You don't want to add bulk or deal with gaping buttons and pulling across the chest. Your best bets are sleek, cropped, tailored jackets with no closure or worn open and notch-collar blazers or tuxedo jackets with a V-neck. Three-quarter sleeves in either case lighten up the upper body since they display narrow forearms and wrists.

## Coats

Swingy, A-shape coats and straight, slim, single-breasted man-tailored topcoats always provide balance. They both allow you to button up easily with no concerns about bulk, even over jackets.

> For very extreme body imbalances, try going monochrome (one color head to toe). Vary the color with tone and texture, but keep the darkest piece where you need to most... on top.

**Don't overdo or undermine your body confidence with clothes that get in the way of success. For example:**

### THE GIRL WHO KNOWS TOO MUCH

ends up looking like a caricature of a fashion victim and twenty pounds heavier. Instead of balancing her body silhouette, she hides what she considers flaws and overdoes it in an effort to appear slimmer and fit. She wears a big, dark, boyfriend blazer over a boxy, man-tailored shirt over a tank with baggy boyfriend jeans rolled at the ankles. She wears a huge, oversized bag to use as a shield to hide her tummy and super-high platform heels 24/7 to make her look taller. She ends up looking like self-confidence is not on her agenda.

### THE GIRL WHO KNOWS TOO LITTLE

wears whatever is in style and figures fashion-forward makes up for body imperfections. She wears tiny shorts with a shapeless embellished tank under a long, droopy cardigan with ankle socks and Miu Miu ankle-strap Mary Janes. Her clothes only emphasize her heavy legs and hips and make her appear clueless and not in control of her style.

# Gretta's Styling Kit

These items are my emergency solutions for last-minute fashion problems. They belong in every woman's closet.

**SILICONE BRA INSERTS**
These are natural-feel gel or silicone pads that resemble chicken cutlets! They can be slipped into the cups of any bra to boost volume on top or bottom of your breasts depending where you need fullness.

**DOUBLE-STICK TAPE** Sticky on both sides, this tape effectively prevents shirt, blouse, and jacket buttons from gaping, keeps wrap dresses and V-necks and halters in place, and can even prevent bra straps from creeping.

**THE BRA CLIP**
A plastic gizmo that pulls your bra straps together midback to hoist up your boobs. In a pinch, I also use a reinforced safety pin or, for smaller breasts that require less heft, a big paper clip. Both have made red-carpet dresses look better when the celeb showed up in the wrong bra.

**THE SUCCESSFUL GIRL** gets it right! She balances trends and style to suit her body silhouette. She wears a belted A-line skirt in a fresh, trendy color, a printed silk top and a cardigan embellished at the neckline to call attention to her upper body and help enhance her heavy lower half without hiding it.

### MINI LINT ROLLER

This tool grabs up dog/cat/human hairs, dandruff, and all the specs and flecks your clothes pick up so they look dry-cleaner fresh. They make wearing back and dark colors worry-free and slip easily into a work or travel bag.

### SMALL TO MEDIUM RUBBER BANDS

 A simple rubber band can help extend a waistband that's become too snug on skirts, jeans, and pants. Just loop around the button, slide through the buttonhole, and loop back around the button. They'll save you on bloated days.

### A PORTABLE SEWING KIT

A mini pack that contains the basic thread colors, needles and pins, small scissors, and a tag-snipper is your backup security team. You can tack up droopy skirt and pant hems  that get caught on heels, sew on loose buttons, and remove irritating labels without leaving a hole in the garment.

### BLACK SHARPIES

These permanent markers save you from nicks and scuffs (especially at the toe and heel) when you can't get to the shoe repair shop or do a polish job yourself. Black is essential, but frankly, any color matched to your shoes works.

after

# THE GRETTA STYLE-OVER

Vanessa lost over 100 lbs in one year on her own through diet and exercise. I helped her rebuild her style from scratch to a more sophisticated look with sleek body grazing pencil skirts, peplum tops, and a youthful overall image. Going blonde and making red lips her signature emphasized her new "movie star" looks.

before

# CHAPTER 7

# THE SUCCESSFUL BEACH BABE, BRIDE, AND BABY

THREE MAJOR LIFE SITUATIONS can throw any Successful Girl's style into a tailspin: pregnancy, wearing a swimsuit, and her own wedding. Sometimes all three coincide! Imagine a three-months-pregnant bride leaving for a Caribbean honeymoon or a post-baby bride (with toddler in tow) at her destination wedding on the beach in Cancun. In this chapter, we have the luxury of solving these three style issues one at a time. Each one presents its own concerns.

Swimsuits mean paring down to reveal your true shape in public. We need those tiny pieces of fabric to do more than camouflage our lady parts, and every girl whether she's a size four or fourteen worries about it.

Getting married—whether it's the first or second time—still means balancing your dream look with the reality of your body or your newfound style. Weddings happen to be the one time when your special one-day look and everyday style may not be in sync—after all, that fantasy dress may have been in your head since your teens!—and that can throw you too. Look at celebs who marry more than once; notice the changes in style between wedding dress #1 and #2!

Having a baby is a major game-changer because your body goes through several transformations. There's your pre-baby trying-to-get-pregnant body (and this can be dually stressful/happy when you may start eating more healthily than usual and more!), your early pregnancy body, full-bloom belly stage, and then your post-baby body. If this is your first pregnancy, you may find these changes a real challenge as you balance style, a multitasking life, work, and the desire to feel confident about the way you look.

I'm going to walk you through each of the three situations with a dress-to-de-stress plan. Let's start with pregnancy and my own multilevel blueprint for success.

These life situations can throw any Successful Girl's style into a tailspin.

# THE SUCCESSFUL GIRL WEARS A SWIMSUIT

WE LOVE CLOTHES FOR THEIR STYLE-BOOSTING, SHAPE-ENHANCING, CONFIDENCE-RAISING ABILITIES. BUT WHEN IT COMES TO WEARING SWIMSUITS, EVERY GIRL HAS ISSUES.... EVEN MODELS AND CELEBRITIES. LET'S BE REALISTIC: THERE'S VERY LITTLE FABRIC, AND IT ALL HAS TO WORK WITH YOUR STYLE, YOUR BODY, AND YOUR LIFESTYLE, TOO. WHETHER YOU SWIM, RUN ON THE BEACH, SURF, PLAY VOLLEYBALL, OR JUST HANG OUT AT THE POOL WITH YOUR KIDS, IT ALL AFFECTS YOUR SWIMSUIT CHOICE.

But it's not all just about the suit. Grooming head-to-toe plays a role in your swim style too. Every Successful Girl spends time waxing or shaving, self-tanning, and getting manicures and pedicures to enhance the swimsuit look. (See more on beauty in chapter 8!) Swimsuit-wearing is always a high-maintenance project.

When choosing a swimsuit, always work from your silhouette first (straight up-and-down, top-heavy, bottom-heavy) and then edit by style (Weekend, Girly, Sophisticated, or Sexy). Whatever you do, never work from a place of fear by focusing on your flaws. Play to and empower your style with what you've learned from working with clothes. Every one of the three body silhouettes can wear two-piece or one-piece suits successfully.

# THE STRAIGHT UP + DOWN SILHOUETTE

*You want to build curves!*
*The #1 mistake this silhouette makes is opting for a*
*plain tank—the kind Olympic swimmers wear.*

You can wear a one-piece suit, but the right ones will have details that create or exaggerate contours. They include one-piece suits with cutouts at the sides, contour seaming, or see-through mesh panels that give an illusion of a two-piece suit. A suit with strategic ruching or draping at the bust, waist, or hip can imply curves, so can a crossover faux wrap style (also called a surplice wrap). Suits with a belt at the waist or hip and one-shoulder asymmetric suits suggest curves, so do those with peplums or ruffles at the hip. Keep the leg cut high whether you prefer a tiny or full-cut bottom on your suit. The last thing you want is a boy-short leg, which give this silhouette a boxy look.

Two-piece suits visually break up straight-up-and-down silhouettes at the middle where they reveal skin. They all need built-in shaping on top to boost your boobs whether the style you choose is strapless, a halter, or one with shoulder straps. A built-in underwire, molded cups, or a twist bandeau can do just that (and this inner structure on top works for your one-piece suits as well).

**WHEN SHE COVERS UP** The straight-up-and-down silhouette chooses a short shift or mini-length tank dress that highlights her long legs and arms.

> Two-piece suits visually break up straight up and down silhouettes at the middle where they reveal skin.

### ■ The Weekend Girl

The Weekend Girl might choose an underwire bikini or strapless underwire one-piece, a tank with ruching, a belt, or a curvy sweetheart neckline.

### ■ The Girly Girl

The Girly Girl might wear a ruffled, floral, striped, or halter bikini with built-in push-up or balcony bra or a colorful one-piece with molded cups.

### ■ The Sophisticated Girl

The Sophisticated Girl may choose a one-shoulder suit or a one-piece with a wide V-neck, or cutouts.

### ■ The Sexy Girl

The Sexy Girl might wear a one-piece with daring side cutouts or a halter bikini with strategic shine.

# THE BOTTOM-HEAVY SILHOUETTE

*Your goal is to create volume and width on top for balance and streamline your bottom half.*

The #1 mistake this silhouette makes is hiding out in a bulky towel sarong, a skirted suit, or full-coverage boy-leg suit. You end up looking matronly and sending an unsuccessful message. Having a generous booty happens to be cool, and managing full thighs and legs just takes a little strategy.

Major contrast between your top and bottom proportions usually means you will look better in a one-piece suit. It's much easier to create a balanced look with a one-piece when the difference is extreme. Look for one-piece suits with wide-set straps and a broad V, scoop, or sweetheart neckline to establish a strong horizontal focal point. One-shoulder suits can be good also since they stretch the torso. Any embellishment at the top of the suit, like a ruffled neckline or hardware on the straps, color blocking, or piping, provides a bonus since they pull attention to your upper body from width below the waist.

If you prefer two-piece suits, or the contrast between your top and bottom is not that extreme, look for brands and specialty stores selling tops and bottoms in different sizes. When it comes to two pieces, a mid-rise bottom just under the belly button with a high leg will be super flattering and works with any top from a tankini to a bra style. Tankinis are actually a whole other option, and the new sexier tops—including tiered ruffled tops and halter—are so different from the frumpy tankinis of the past.

No matter what suit you choose, the details make all the difference. Keep the leg cut high and angled up to create a longer, slimmer line at the thigh and hip. Fill out your boobs with a suit that has molded or contoured underwire cups. This lifts the full part of your breasts higher on your chest so you gain midriff space (and don't sag!). By stretching your top half, you balance your lower body. You can even wear a strapless suit if the top is curved (not cut straight across!) and has a built-in bra. Halter suits can be a perfect option, especially if the top has curve-boosting light padding, draping, or ruching. Strategic color-blocking works for either one- or two-piece suits if the top is brighter or lighter than the bottom. Look for suits with extra draping or ruching from the waist down (there are plenty) to camouflage a tummy bulge if that contributes to your specific body issues aside from the bottom-heavy silhouette.

**WHEN SHE COVERS UP** The Successful Girl with a bottom-heavy silhouette wears a sheer, long sarong that is fluid…and never all day long. She has body and style confidence to carry her through.

> The #1 mistake this silhouette makes is hiding out in a bulky towel sarong, a skirted suit, or full-coverage boy-leg suit.

### ■ The Weekend Girl

The Weekend Girl might choose a bicolor bikini with contoured cups, lighter top, and darker bottom or a two-piece with high cut brief bottom.

### ■ The Girly Girl

The Girly Girl might wear a bikini or tankini with a tiered or ruffle top or a print halter-neck one-piece with ruching.

### ■ The Sophisticated Girl

The Sophisticated Girl might wear a classic, one-piece scoop, with cutout, or draped-neck in classy black.

### ■ The Sexy Girl

The Sexy Girl might wear a halter-top bikini one-piece with attention getting details like ruffles at the bust or bows or a super low-cut double-scoop tank in a metallic fabric.

# THE TOP-HEAVY SILHOUETTE

*The more extreme the contrast between top and bottom, the more strategic your choices need to be.*

Your silhouette is the opposite of bottom-heavy, but some of the same logic about balance applies to you too. Girls with big boobs tend to hunch over and wear a T-shirt or tank over their suit. Time to stop all that and find the right swimsuits with enough support that are still sexy. I'm not suggesting a string bikini with a triangle top. Just don't limit yourself to high-coverage suits.

Heavy breasts that are larger than a C cup need suits (whether one- or two-piece styles) with some form of full inner bra structure to stabilize things. Molded and contoured cups with the lift of a good support bra are essential and amazing on this silhouette, especially structured halters with an adjustable tie so you control lift. Some of the best halters in this category have a retro 40s look with wide-spaced, sturdy straps and a twist or pinch pleat detail front and center where the cups meet.

Medium, full breasts also rock in tie-neck halters with underwire cup support, a wider band, or a center ring for separation. If you love two-piece suits and want a more balanced look, choose low rise foldover bikini bottoms or skirtinis (low-rise, minskirt bikini bottoms) and tie-side bottoms. They look sexy and make your two halves look evenly proportioned.

One-piece suits with plunge-V necklines and scoop tanks have a *Baywatch* appeal on top-heavy girls, so don't pass these up if you have the confidence to show some cleavage. But still opt for some inner help with lightly padded or foam-lined cups, and be prepared for eye contact. One-shoulder suits, V one-piece suits with crossover draping or a side-wrap effect, and two-piece styles with a full-coverage molded bra and wide straps spaced far apart are other good choices when

you want more coverage and less attention. And again, colorblocking works when the bottom is brighter or lighter than the top. Here's how the top-heavy swimsuit choices might work:

**WHEN SHE COVERS UP** the Successful Girl with a top-heavy silhouette wears a sheer mini tunic or wrap beach dress in a silky fabric.

## Time to stop hiding and find the right swimsuits with enough support that are still sexy.

### ■ The Weekend Girl

The Weekend Girl may choose a one-piece or two-piece halter with underwire cups, or a twist-ring to keep the girls lifted.

### ■ The Girly Girl

The Girly Girl may wear a one-piece retro halter with built-in bra and ruched cups, a two-piece skirtini suit that diverts the eye downwards, or a bikini with a contoured bra or halter for support.

### ■ The Sophisticated Girl

The Sophisticated Girl might wear a one-shoulder suit with inner bra or a ruched one-piece with lower body detail.

### ■ The Sexy Girl

The Sexy Girl might wear a scoopy tank with an extra super-low back in a look-at-me color or print or a plunge halter bikini in an always sexy black.

# FOR ALL SILHOUETTES

Whether you're post-baby or have a flabby midriff from weight loss or gain, don't back off from wearing a sexy suit. A control suit made with a higher percentage of Lycra or spandex can suck in excess bulging and sag, especially in the tummy area, and give you a firm look just like a piece of shapewear does under your clothes. Certain brands like Miraclesuit and Spanx specialize in swim-shape suits with extra control panels built through the middle and are worth the splurge. Other everyday suit brands offer styles with ruching straight down the center of the suit or an asymmetric draped section across the tummy for extra help. Any one or combo of these gets an additional boost from diversionary use of colorblocking, all-over prints with a swirly look, low-contrast prints or those on a dark background, and matte fabrics. You'll want to avoid rigid uniform patterns like stripes and geometrics, prints on light backgrounds, and shiny fabrics that maximize shape.

# THE SUCCESSFUL GIRL GETS MARRIED

WEDDINGS, BIG EVENTS, AND SPECIAL-OCCASION PARTIES LIKE BLACK-TIE GALAS ARE NOT SOMETHING YOU DO EVERY DAY. YOUR OWN WEDDING IS THE ONE TIME WHEN YOU CAN POSSIBLY LET GO OF YOUR IDEAL STYLE AND GO WITH YOUR FANTASY BECAUSE THEY MAY NOT MATCH UP! DON'T LET YOUR DREAM WEDDING GET DERAILED BY A TOTAL FOCUS ON REALITY, BUT KEEP AN OPEN MIND. A CINDERELLA-STYLE WEDDING DRESS AT 42 WHEN YOU'RE 5'1" MAY NOT BE THE BEST IDEA.

By the time you've read this book and gotten through this chapter, even your dream wedding look might have changed to one that's really in sync with your style, spirit, and body. But let's bring it all back to your original inspiration board for a minute. You've identified your style and made it your own from looking at photos that resonated for you. I'm willing to bet somewhere in that dream wedding look is the style you discovered for your own.

Celeb weddings are, of course, a can't-miss opportunity to see this theory in action. However, even then, brides seem to go for the fantasy look in wedding #1 and come back to own their real style in wedding #2. See Mariah Carey and Audrey Hepburn to get the picture. One of my early jobs in retail was working at a bridal shop. I basically served coffee to clients and helped locate samples from the stock for brides to try on. But my real training came from watching and listening to the saleswomen (who had all been in this business for decades) sell. The bride always arrived with an entourage in tow and sure of what she wanted. After letting her try on 100 dresses that fit her "dream" but didn't work, the clever saleswoman would say, "Would you just try one dress for me?" Of course, it was far from the bride's original concept, but it usually worked like magic. Stay open-minded—you may be happily surprised.

## The Weekend Girl

If you're a Weekend Girl, you're attracted to anything flowy, bohemian, or vintagey, from thirties flapper to Victorian summer whites. Take a look at the wedding gowns of Lilly Allen, Nicole Kidman (who went Victorian for Keith Urban), and Heidi Montag (wedding #2).

**GRETTA'S STYLE SECRET:** Any gown that has a retro feeling, turn-of-the-century elegance, or Old Hollywood glam to it is essentially romantic. Keep your hair feminine and loose, in a low, soft knot with tendrils, or softly waved. Pearls always look right, and don't add a fussy look to the nostalgia—they play up the sweetness without being too cloying.

## The Girly Girl

If you're a Girly Girl, you're attracted to "princess" looks, feminine styles with ruffles, frills, frou, and lace—the bigger and bolder the better. Check out the gowns on Anne Hathaway (who ordinarily is a Sophisticated Girl), Kate Middleton, Ivanka Trump, Victoria Beckham, Salma Hayek, Chelsea Clinton, Avril Lavigne, and Gwen Stefani (OK, even though it was dip-dyed pink at the bottom).

**GRETTA'S STYLE SECRET:** Fairy-tale dresses are fun to dance in and joyful to wear. They can be simple, floaty ball gowns with a structured bodice and full skirt or highly embellished with layers of tulle, cascading ruffles, and crystals. Avoid too much extra accessorizing here with lots of jewelry—this is a youthful look, and all you need are beautiful, delicate shoes and long hair swept up in a tousled bun or tumbling down with volume and shine. Another great variation of the girly dress is empire with a tiny pouf sleeve and decolleté neckline (kind of like Shakespeare's Juliet), though it emphasizes the bosom rather than the waist if that's your asset.

## The Sophisticated Girl

If you're a Sophisticated Girl, you're attracted to simple, elegant slips and sheaths with a luxurious look, like the gowns worn by Carolyn Bessette, Cindy Crawford, Megan Fox, Alicia Keys, Eva Longoria, and Jenna Bush.

**GRETTA'S STYLE SECRET:** Tailored gowns that hug the body's curves look totally contemporary. They can be clean and almost sculptural and have minimal embellishment like beaded or jeweled straps or a draped front and back neckline. Keep the minimalist theme with simple hair and tapered-toe shoes or strappy sandals. You can always add subtle embellishment with a beaded shrug or bolero for coverage during the ceremony.

## The Sexy Girl

If you're a Sexy Girl, you're still attracted to body-hugging, mermaid-style corsets and halters, maybe even a mini for your wedding! Take a look at Hilary Duff, Khloe Kardashian, Mariah Carey (wedding #2), Yoko Ono in mini (to marry John Lennon), Audrey Hepburn in mini (to marry husband #2), Christina Aguilera, and Fergie.

**GRETTA'S STYLE SECRET:** The back of your gown may be daringly low, a cowl or draped, or with a black velvet bow above your derriere. Or you might be strapless, showing off toned arms and shoulders as you heat up the dance floor. Your idea of a wedding dress might even be a gold mermaid dress covered with shimmery sequins or a one-shoulder, vanilla lace, knee-length sheath. These dresses are anything but traditional and can handle statement shoes (like jeweled cage booties) or major sparkly earrings to highlight a bare neckline and updo.

# GRETTA'S HOW-TO-LOOK-GREAT-FOR-YOUR-WEDDING RECIPE

*I guarantee every Successful Girl can follow my five-step plan confident she'll look and feel like an Oscar nominee start to finish.*

Every bride wants to look absolutely delicious for the wedding and all the moments leading up to the big day, including the engagement party, bridal shower, bachelorette party, and rehearsal dinner. You'll also want to keep the look going through the honeymoon, because every moment start to finish will be recorded on film or video forever. I guarantee every Successful Girl can follow my five-step plan confident she'll look and feel like an Oscar nominee start to finish. In fact, the wedding-prep secrets I share with you here come straight from my work as a stylist and beauty expert helping celeb clients prepare for their own events.

## 1. Start prepping early.

If you decide to add highlights, cut bangs, or layer your hair, do it three to six months before the wedding. This gives you plenty of time to love-it or leave-it before the big day. Work on making your smile look its healthiest. Get any dental work out of the way, and go for a pro whitening procedure or start a serious at-home whitening routine with drugstore strips. Eat healthy (starving yourself won't help your skin, hair, or nails look their best), and work out regularly to tone up and feel good about your body no matter what your size or shape. If your hair is dry or damaged, start weekly moisturizing masks to reboot shine and body. Get trims to eliminate splits. If your hair is frizz-prone (and you prefer a smooth look) and your wedding is in the summer, a humid climate, or a tropical destination, talk to your stylist about a salon keratin treatment for good-hair-day security. See a dermatologist about skin concerns like chest or back breakouts that may cause anxiety for the big day or parties leading up to it. Consider nail wraps if you're a nibbler so your hands look beautiful and elegant. Treat yourself to spa facials and body treatments if you can, or follow my at-home spa strategies for waxing, polishing, and getting skin bare-able in chapter 8.

## 2. Two weeks before showtime.

Get your final dress fitting since your weight may have changed a bit. Make sure you have a makeup/hair dress rehearsal (with and without the headpiece and veil for the hair part) so there are no last-minute decisions. Wax and get any last-minute treatments like brow shaping, lash extensions, or fresh highlights three to five days before the wedding. Some girls stay red and puffy for days post-waxing or experience some subtle sensitivity. Get a salon spray-tan two or three days before, since it will last a week and you can touch up with a gradual self-tanner on your honeymoon. Don't go more than two shades up from your natural skin tone. It can hide stretch marks, veins, and even help contour areas like your stomach, thighs, booty, and upper arms. The technician goes darker on these areas for a whittled look. (Celebs do this all the time for TV, films, and the red carpet.) Drink tons of water, eat fresh fish, veggies, and fruit, and stop eating sugar, bread, pasta, cheese, soda, and alcohol (except for your own parties!). If you can squeeze in a salon massage or two: That and a soothing manicure/pedicure can help you relax in the two pre-wedding ramp-up days.

## 3. Stay true to your look for the wedding.

Going too far from the way you usually appear for the wedding celebration is always a mistake. This means no exaggerated makeup (like wearing red lips or smudgy late-night eyes for the first time ever), new haircuts, or major hair color or hair changes that don't reflect your own style. You want to look like the best everyday version of you, only enhanced. You can always save the killer lips, hair extensions, or sexy black eye makeup for the bachelorette party! Do yourself a favor and book a makeup pro for the wedding, and a hairstylist, too, if you can swing it, or someone skilled in both or at least the makeup half. You can always dash to a salon on the day of for a blowout and style, or DIY if your hair is a simple knot or bun. Do pale pink or nude nails—bold or trendy colors take away from the look and can be distracting in photos.

## 4. Do makeup that lasts and looks good on camera.

You want to look fresh all day/night through. What you don't want is to sweat off your makeup dancing or to reflect too much light so your skin looks greasy. Use a makeup primer on your face and eyes to create an invisible, clingy base and help makeup last. Follow with foundation set with loose powder. Pay attention to the T-zone, where skin tends to get oily, especially at the creases around the nostrils. You want to create an even, flawless, semimatte look. Stash oil-blotting sheets in your bag—better than adding more powder later, which can look cakey after multiple touch-up applications. A touch of shimmer can be flattering on top of cheekbones or lids, but avoid too much sparkle or highlighter since the camera picks up anything light-reflecting as shine and maximizes it. So watch the lip gloss too. You may want a creamy pencil, tinted balm, or sheer lipstick or stain. Play up your eyes. This is a safe zone for emphasis since your mouth will be busy kissing, drinking, and laughing. False lashes are a smart, easy move and make every Successful Girl's eyes look twice their size, happy, and alert (even after too much wine at the rehearsal dinner and champagne at the wedding). This may be the time to use a waterproof black mascara if you tear up easily—black streaks are not easy to repair!

## 5. Prepare for trouble.

Anticipate a problem before it happens. Make sure you know how to manage the bustle easily with the tiny buttons/hooks and eyes or snaps to tuck it up after the ceremony so you can maneuver around. Have a tinted pimple treatment for last-minute zits, a makeup touch-up kit (with cotton swabs, concealer, extra lash glue, your lip/eye makeup, and blotting sheets), a mini perfume spray, breath mints, a disposable toothbrush, a safety pin or two, and baby wipes to freshen up fast and get out any stains quickly on that white dress.

# THE SUCCESSFUL GIRL HAS A BABY

LOOKING YOUR BEST WHEN YOUR BODY IS NO LONGER TOTALLY UNDER YOUR CONTROL TAKES STRATEGY. SUCCESSFUL GIRLS GET PREGNANT TOO BUT KNOW HOW TO KEEP THEIR STYLE AND EDGE! EVERY GIRL THINKS ABOUT PREGNANCY IN TERMS OF WEIGHT GAIN, BUT THE TRUTH IS, YOUR SHAPE AND ATTITUDE CHANGE WAY BEFORE YOUR BELLY POPS.

Even at the very beginning when you're in the just-trying stage, your style begins to lean toward comfort. Some women are told by their doctors to gain weight as a way of improving their chances, especially if they're strict diet-and-exercise junkies. Gaining a few, whether you're planning or already in early pregnancy, can immediately make you feel less confident and unsure about what to wear. My first tip is to manage the mental change ASAP. Yes, your body is going to evolve in a new way, and there are new solutions to deal with all the transformations.

*Yes, your body is going to evolve in a new way, and there are new solutions to deal with all the transformations.*

# THE GOTTA-HAVES

## This is your baby confidence kit

SOME WOMEN JUMP STRAIGHT INTO DRESS-
ING PREGNANT RIGHT FROM THE DECISION
TO TRY. OTHERS RESIST GOING PUBLIC OR
MAKING STYLE ADJUSTMENTS AS LONG AS
POSSIBLE. ONCE THINGS ARE OUT IN THE
OPEN, EVERYONE AT WORK—YOUR BOSS,
YOUR COLLEAGUES, YOUR CLIENTS AND CUS-
TOMERS—WILL CELEBRATE YOUR HAPPI-
NESS. BUT YOU WANT TO BE CLEAR TO ALL
THAT YOU'RE ON YOUR GAME AND WILL
MAINTAIN PRODUCTIVITY, ATTENTION, AND
WORK SUCCESS WITHOUT ANY COMPRO-
MISES. LOOKING GREAT THROUGHOUT YOUR
ENTIRE PREGNANCY — THE GETTING-
PREGNANT STAGE, EARLY PREGNANCY (BUT
NOT YET SHOWING), THE NINE-MONTH SAGA,
AND POST-BABY—IS IMPORTANT FOR YOUR
SELF-ESTEEM AND YOUR RELATIONSHIPS
WITH EVERYONE IN YOUR LIFE. START OFF
KNOWING WHICH ITEMS WILL MAKE THE
MOST DIFFERENCE.

## 1. A NEW SUPPORT BRA IN THE RIGHT SIZE

Bust size changes dra-
matically over a preg-
nancy. Right from the
start, your boobs will
be bigger and more
sensitive than normal
period-bloat fullness
and tenderness. A
jump to two sizes + is
typical, and a new bra
will allow you to stay in your usual clothes longer.
Each of the three body silhouettes will be affected
by this initial change. A straight up-and-down silhouette benefits from and enjoys her new curves.
She'll get enough support from a convertible-strap
or racerback bra with light foam fill. The top-heavy
silhouette regains control of her growing ample
chest with a minimizer or full-figure contour bra.
Minimizers are specially designed to compress
and redistribute delicate breast tissue to reduce
the look of your chest. Contour bras are pre-
molded to contain, shape, and lift. Both bras help
top-heavy shapes compensate for increased size
and weight so sag and spillage don't become a
problem. The bottom-heavy silhouette gains a
more balanced look as her breasts go up in size.
She benefits from an underwire balcony bra that
lifts her newly full breasts or a molded bra with
pre-shaped cups. Go to a department store or
specialty shop with a professional bra fitter on
staff.

**BEST CHOICE** A supportive, breast stabilizing
bra that lifts the fullest part of your boobs level
with your underarm.

## 2. A TUMMY BAND OR WAIST EXTENDER

Stay in your usual jeans, skirts, and pants as long as possible with one of these options. A tummy band is a stretchy, wide, knit band (think super-size stretch hairband) that covers the waistband of your partially unbuttoned jeans, skirts, and pants before, during, and after pregnancy. It reads as a layering piece and provides ease and security when you can't zip up or button up all the way. Waistband extenders are a simple button-and-loop gadget that attach to your usual jeans/skirt/pant button. They add anywhere from a half inch to two inches of room. (FYI, they come in handy when you're bloated and not pregnant too!) Both gadgets keep you wearing your regular or maternity-size bottoms without having to buy fresh ones with every new couple of pounds gained. They also make the post-baby transition back into your wardrobe easier. You can even send your favorite jeans to Belly Jeans (belly-jeans.com) and for about $25 get a stretch band added.

**BEST CHOICE** Bellaband (ingridandisabel.com) $28, in black, white, and nude, which looks like a layering piece, or the Tummy Sleeve by Motherhood ($16.98, www.motherhood.com).

## 3. A MATERNITY SHAPER PANTY

An upgrade of your usual mid-thigh biker shaper, this nylon/spandex support piece holds you in, provides back and belly support, and smooths the line between baby bump, hips, thighs, and derriere. Maternity shapewear is ideal from the middle to end of your pregnancy. It makes you feel firm and shapely in a good way and prevents dress fabrics from riding up.

**BEST CHOICE** A nude or black shaper panty with a cotton gusset like the Secret Fit Shaper Panty ($16.98, www.motherhood.com).

## 4. MATERNITY JEANS

Eventually you will want a pair or two. Stick with your style preference here—anything from Weekend Girl's vintage wash to Girly Girl's pink and floral prints, Sophisticated Girl's dark denim to Sexy Girl's stretch black. All are available in fitted, skinny, straight, and slim ankle-cropped maternity jeans from brands like AG Jeans, 7 For All Mankind, Joe's Jeans, and Paige Premium and J Brand at A Pea in the Pod ( www.apeainthepod.com). Liz Lange for Target also has great low-cost maternity jeans. Pair them with wedges for height and comfort or flat boots.

**BEST CHOICE** Your favorite brand in a skinny or fitted straight-leg style to give you a slim, confident base for long tees, tunics, and floaty tops. Stretch denim provides the most comfort.

## 5. STRETCH JERSEY DRESSES

Show your baby bump in a clingy dress or a stretch pencil and clingy tee. It's the new way to do pregnancy. No more hiding under stiff structured shifts! Wear your jerseys with bare legs and peep-toe wedges or tights and boots.

**BEST CHOICE** A pull-on, body-hugging jersey dress in your favorite color.

## 6. A MAXI DRESS

When you're in those last two months or while settling in at home with your new baby, one or two maxis are a gift to yourself. Very L.A. and chic, you can relax in sandals or wedges with a pair of hoops or dangly earrings and feel pretty confident.

**BEST CHOICE** A loose, strapless, or empire printed dress that floats over the body or a rayon/spandex jersey knit, sleeveless column that molds to your body.

## 7. LONG, STRETCH-KNIT DESIGNER MATERNITY TEES

When you belly bulge pops, your usual tees will be too short. Look for tees in supple, opaque, modal/spandex jersey or cotton/modal blends. They're worth the splurge for the fit and look since you'll be wearing them over and over with jeans, maternity leggings, and yoga pants. Splendid, Michael Stars, Bailey 44, and Vince make the best.

**BEST CHOICE** Scoop or V-necks in supple matte fabrics that hug your silhouette and cover your belly totally. Test by you stretching your arms above your head. Black for sure and gray, stripes, and your favorite wardrobe colors.

## 8. DROP-YOKE YOGA PANTS

I wanted to live in my sweatpants 24/7 when trying to get pregnant. That desire for comfort is powerful at this very emotional time whether you're doing the natural thing or getting some in-vitro help. Stretch-jersey yoga pants feel just as good but are not sloppy like sweats. They provide a slim base for tops during downtime, parenting activities, or running errands. During pregnancy, black maternity yoga pants are an essential update you'll want to buy.

**BEST CHOICE** Black, cut higher in back, lower in front, and narrow through the thighs with a smooth, wide, flat waistband (some fold over for more coverage and comfort). This is one basic you'll rely on nine+ months.

## 9. WEDGES

You're going to still want height and a leg-lengthening look, but comfort counts. Let wedges outrank heels for now. Remember you're balancing body weight that's very different from your usual body proportions. A wedge offers more support to your entire sole and arches... and back!

**BEST CHOICE**
Sexy wedges that can sub for your favorite killer heels or boots. Avoid ankle-wrap and ankle-strap shoe versions since ankles, feet, and legs swell during pregnancy. The Weekend Girl may choose an espadrille style or cork-sole wedges; the Girly Girl may go for peep-toe platform wedges in colorful patent or suede; the Sophisticated Girl will want narrow contoured wedges that stand in for polished pumps; and the Sexy Girl will love metallic peep-toe wedges that let her edgy pedi show. Wedge boots provide stability and height for colder weather. Look for rubber soles that can get you through icy/rainy/stormy days without slipping.

## 10. WRAP DRESSES AND DRAPE-FRONT CARDIGANS

These two versatile items provide lots of options and work in a similar way. Your usual wrap dresses provide body definition and enable you to adjust fit for boobs and belly as you grow (and shrink back post-baby). As you pop, maternity wrap dresses work the same way and provide a great, polished, 24/7 work/evening solution. Drapey front cardigans (also called cascade cardigans) are cut longer in front to swing and/or wrap in multiple ways. They look great over simple tees or pull-on jersey dresses. You can tie them in front, wrap and tie in back, toss one end over a shoulder, or simply let the open edges dangle in graceful folds for coverage and style flexibility.

**BEST CHOICE**
A wrap dress in a swirly print (for additional camouflage or fun) and a light, draped cardigan that works for day or night in your favorite color or black.

# GRETTA'S PREGNANCY STYLE GUIDE TO SUCCESS

Some girls barely look pregnant at six months, while other look six months pregnant at three. Every pregnancy is different, and the way your body changes will be different, but in general here's the map of what to expect and how to navigate the route with style intact.

## 0–4 months

Most everything in your closet should still work, especially if you upgrade your bras. If you spend on anything now, new bras are it. The right ones will enable you to hold off buying clothes. Don't switch into a pregnancy look too early. Wear what you have until you no longer can, and hold back on shopping till the next stage. Since your breasts are the big giveaway, be wary of button-down shirts and blouses. Wrap tops and narrow tunics are better-choice confidence-boosters. Wear them over a slim-bottom pencil skirt, fitted jeans, or narrow, straight pants. Right now, it's all about managing your boobs, not your belly. If you're still having serious top issues (even with new bras), wear dresses. The simplicity of one-piece dressing streamlines your body for a more uniform look. Dresses that are strategically color blocked (darker on top) or have an all-over, small, random print provide an extra diversion. Successful Girls who are struggling with morning sickness know any dress in a fresh pop of color will send an "up" message at work. Wearing more color now is a great ally as your new hormonal changes kick in. Start using your bellyband or waistband extenders too with your usual bottoms to give you a little extra room.

## 5–7 months

This is the sweet spot. You're over morning sickness, your bump is defined and proportionate to your boobs, and you're blossoming. Your body temperature is up, and so is your energy. Your hair looks healthy and glossy, skin is glowing, and nails are in great shape due to all those changing hormones. You're into your pregnancy look and rolling with it. Now's the time to add maternity stretch yoga pants, maternity jeans and leggings, and some new, longer tops to your wardrobe if your belly is growing quickly. Stretchy fitted dresses—knits, jerseys, and sweaterdresses—that show your shape keep your look sexy and modern. Even if you work in a serious office, embrace your Successful Girl style and flaunt it while showing you are still efficient and pumping on all cylinders. Yahoo! CEO Marissa Mayer was hired to be the company's top executive when six months pregnant!

## 8–9 months

Once I hit eight months, I popped—no waist, no curve definition. I was carrying as if I had twins, and my extra baby-weight gain topped fifty percent of my normal total body weight. You're probably going to be uncomfortable at this stage—fatigued and can't sleep, and your legs and ankles may swell. I had to buy stretchy boots and wedges a size up from my shoe size to compensate. For many women at this point, your back, shoulders, and arms are bigger too, so work jackets may not fit—even worn open! If you're still working, add few fresh pieces just to get you through, like an unstructured jacket and a new stretchy dress. Your rings may not fit. Light hoops and skinny stacked bangles can add a little sparkle without weight. I was fortunate to go through this period in summer and lived in maxis, pretty caftans at home, loose, floaty bohemian tops with leggings, my long designer tees, and draped cardigans.

## After the baby

This is when you've checked out of work and are taking care of the baby 24/7. In the first several weeks, you'll still be wearing some of your smaller early maternity clothes and getting into a nursing bra, camisoles, and crossover tops that allow you to nurse and pump. Enjoy taking care of and bonding with baby, but don't slip into looking sloppy or getting careless about style. You may feel overwhelmed and emotionally challenged as your hormones shift again and your attention is refocused on mothering. Like many women, I had an emergency C-section. This left me feeling like I was hit by a truck. My body needed extra recovery time, but every post-baby girl needs to adjust and adapt her style to compensate for body changes. Expect it, and prepare for it. And be sure to make time for yourself—a bubble bath, good skin care, a manicure. During this time, you can think about how your new life will impact your routine, lifestyle, and looks.

## Gretta-quette

When six months pregnant with my son, Kai, I attended the Emmys wearing a beautiful, strapless, vintage tea-length Dior couture dress. I had bought it at Michael's, a NYC consignment shop, three months earlier. By the time it came to strut the red carpet, my belly was hitting where the dress's hip was supposed to go. Getting creative, I just pulled it up, adjusted the zipper a bit, and looked sexy and radiant in my elegantly transformed gown. Then at nine months, I appeared on air for QVC at Super Saturday in the Hamptons on Long Island. This is a star-studded benefit/garage sale of sorts for the Ovarian Cancer Research Fund held every summer by the fashion industry. I wore a long, strapless maxi dress and made it through despite the ninety-nine degree heat, sixty extra pounds of baby weight, and swollen face, eyes, and feet.

# THE OMG! MOMENT

Some women decide to be a stay-at-home mom, work from home, work part-time, or change careers after having a new baby. Others go back to work full-time and even then have to get up to speed on projects and plans.

If you're breast-feeding, your breasts are leaking and full, so nursing bras and tops that permit easy feeding are great. Try wraps and stretchy tanks with low scoops. If you're back at work, pumping may now be part of your office restroom routine. In most cases, your body has not shrunk back to normal (but if it has bounced back instantly, good for you!). Your hair may be shedding and your skin unstable as your body slows from turbo-gear into mommy mode.

It's time to march into your closet and get a baseline read on what you can wear. If you're at home and have ten to twenty pounds to lose or your boobs are still large, wear yoga pants and a top

around the house. This between-time is a short window, so keep it simple. Dresses are an easy solution, especially those magical wrap styles if you're back at work and pumping. Stretchy knit tops and pencils, black or dark fitted jeans with boots, and a long blazer are fine, for example, too. Gradually your boobs will recede, and your silhouette will regain definition (even if you're not the same size), so you can resume your Successful Girl style. This may even be the time to spend on a few new items to enhance your wardrobe. Take a look at your strategy wheel priorities and body. Sometimes your size changes for good as well, adding a few curves or dropping extra pounds with the baby weight. All becomes part of your evolving blueprint.

> This might be the time to spend on a few new items to enhance your wardrobe.

# THE GRETTA STYLE-OVER

Aida was a first time mom at 43. When we met she was in her eighth month and having trouble dressing with style around her last lap of pregnancy. I put her in a clingy jersey dress in electric blue to recharge her energy and sexy style spirit.

*before*

*after*

# CHAPTER 8

# THE BUSINESS OF BEAUTY

**AS A SALON AND SPA OWNER,** I believe in professional guidance and treatments whether you go regularly, occasionally, once a year, or only for special occasions. On the other hand, I know the right, consistent, at-home care is just as important in creating and maintaining a successful look. Your DIY plan can certainly be spa-inspired, and I'll show you how. As a beauty business owner, I invest only in the brands, products, and treatments that guarantee successful results for my clients. In this chapter, you'll see only products and tools I know are reliable at the luxurious end and at affordable prices.

So what is successful beauty? It's confidence in knowing you look your best 24/7, not wasting time or money on products and regimens that are wrong for you, and having the flexibility to keep updating yourself without losing style. Fashion goes a long way toward establishing your iconic style, but beauty is a major component in the overall success of that look. This may sound funny, but you speak from your face—it's where people focus their attention. Making eye contact and smiling are an essential strategy, but making the most of your appearance is too.

If someone took away my T3 blow-dryer, my Mason Pearson brush, and my high-end spa products, I would have a meltdown. Quality tools and products really make a difference, but the groundbreaking ingredients and delivery systems in them are available at every price. However, you really

have to know exactly what to look for when navigating the thousands of options out there. I'm in the process of building my own beauty brand, so I try everything and know the business of beauty goes beyond what is in that bottle or box. In this final chapter, I'm going to help you define exactly which products and beauty tips will have the most impact on your looks. You'll learn where to splurge—for some women it's a red designer lipstick, for others it's pricey moisturizer—and where to cut corners.

> *Successful beauty is the confidence in knowing you look your best 24/7.*

This might surprise you, but I'm one of the few beauty and style experts with a cosmetology license. This means I can actually cut, color, and style hair and do facials, head-to-toe skincare treatments (including waxing), makeup, brows, and nails. I've worked on tens of thousands of real women like you. Even on makeover TV segments, I'm not afraid to get my hands dirty. Sometimes I actually do the transformation myself and sometimes I work with a team, but I'm in the trenches, not just a "talking head." I love the whole process.

# HOW TO HAVE SUCCESSFUL SKIN HEAD-TO-TOE

SUCCESSFUL SKIN IS FRESH, HEALTHY, AND GLOWING, AND IT'S ACHIEVABLE NO MATTER WHAT YOUR AGE, SKIN TONE, OR COMPLEXION ISSUES. EVERY SUCCESSFUL GIRL NEEDS TO BUILD A BEAUTY ROUTINE STARTING WITH A BASE OF SIMPLE, QUICK, EFFICIENT SKIN CARE. WHILE THE SECRET TO GREAT SKIN IS STEADY DIY CARE EVERY DAY OF THE WEEK, MY ULTIMATE STRATEGY FOR YOU WOULD INCLUDE A BOOSTER SHOT AT THE SALON WHEN NEEDED.

Skin is in a constant state of evolution and shows the effects of current everyday life and your past. This is most visible in facial skin, where lack of sleep, a poor diet or habits, genes, your current skin care, and skin-neglect history reveal themselves.

In this section, I've broken down facial skin into two categories—troubled skin and lived-in skin—as a guide toward your best products and rituals. Troubled skin includes complexions that are breakout prone, oily, sensitive, blotchy, or bothered by rosacea. Maybe you had acne as a teen or have blemish issues now due to hormonal changes, medications, stress, or diet deficiencies. Lived-in skin, on the other hand, shows the effects of too much sun exposure, tanning salon sun beds, smoking, alcohol, or heredity, with dark circles and discolorations or broken capillaries. If you're a bit older, your skin may be showing signs of age with lines, brown spots, or sagging around your eyes or under the chin. Whether your complexion is troubled or lived-in, you'll need the right cleanser, an exfoliator, and a moisturizer to start—the core steps to quality skin—and then some extras. Here's how to select the best products for you.

*I'm going to help you define exactly which products and beauty tips will have the most impact on your looks.*

# THE GOTTA-HAVES

**This is your successful skin kit for face and body**

## 1. MAKEUP REMOVER

If you wear full makeup or sunscreen, choose a separate makeup-removal step in the evening prior to cleansing to make sure all pigment is gone from face and eyes. Leftover makeup, mascara, and sunscreen residue can clog pores or cause irritation and prevent overnight treatments from working effectively. Choose 2-in-1 wipes, balms, or oils that remove both eye and face makeup. Disposable premoistened wipes with built-in cleanser are not greasy and make additional cleansing unnecessary. They're ideal for quick makeup redos and travel.

### BEST CHOICE FOR CREAM/BALM REMOVER

Clinique Take the Day Off Cleansing Balm ($28.50), Bobbi Brown Hydrating Rich Cream Cleanser ($28)

### BEST CHOICE FOR REMOVER WIPES

Neutrogena Makeup Remover Cleansing Towelettes ($6), Almay Makeup Remover Towelettes ($6)

## 2. A FACE CLEANSER FOR YOUR SKIN ISSUES

Getting your skin clean of dirt, oil, and impurities is an important a.m. and p.m. routine to never skip.

### BEST CHOICE FOR TROUBLED SKIN

Murad Clarifying Cleanser ($26), Kate Somerville Detox Daily Cleanser ($32), Peter Thomas Roth Anti-Aging Cleansing Gel ($35) or Peter Thomas Roth Beta Hydroxy Acid 2 % Acne Wash ($35), Neutrogena Naturals Acne Foaming Scrub ($9)

### BEST CHOICE FOR LIVED-IN SKIN

Fresh Soy Face Cleanser ($38), Clarins One-Step Exfoliating Facial Cleanser with Orange Extract ($35), Dior Gentle Cleansing Milk with Velvet Peony Extract ($33), Cetaphil Daily Facial Cleanser ($12)

## 3. A FACIAL EXFOLIATOR

A scrub, polish, peel, mask, or face wash with physical or chemical exfoliating ingredients buffs away flakes, dead cells, and all the junk sitting on top of our skin that prevents it from looking its brightest. Physical exfoliating facial scrubs and polishers include sugar or microbeads. Chemical exfoliating masks or peels rely on fruit enzymes or AHAs. They dissolve dead cells on the surface of the skin in minutes without any abrasive action. Peels are usually pads or gels that use enzymes or acids like glycolic, malic, lactic, and salicylic. A sonic exfoliating brush or even a soft, manual face brush turns any liquid, milky, cream, gel, or foam cleanser into an exfoliating treatment too.

**BEST CHOICE** June Jacobs Perfect Pumpkin Enzyme Polish ($60), June Jacobs Sensitive Formula Mandarin Polishing Beads ($44), June Jacobs Fresh Sugar Face Polish ($55), Peter Thomas Roth FIRMx Peeling Gel ($48), The Clarisonic Mia 2 ($14), Shiseido Skincare Cleansing Massage brush ($25), Aveeno Positively Radiant Skin Brightening Daily Scrub ($7), Simple Exfoliating Facial Wipes($6), Simple Smoothing Facial Scrub ($7)

## 4. A MOISTURIZER FOR YOUR SKIN NEEDS

Every Successful Girl needs a moisturizer regardless of skin concerns. Choose a day cream with built-in sunscreen, or a day/night moisturizer that does double duty, or separate moisturizers for day and night depending on your lifestyle, needs, and preferences. Choose oil-free formulas for acne prone or oily skin and more hydrating formulas with light emollients, extra humectants, and proven de-agers for lived-in skin.

### BEST CHOICE FOR TROUBLED SKIN

Olay Age Defying Sensitive Skin Day Lotion SPF 15 ($12), Clinique Moisture Surge Extended Thirst Relief ($37)

### BEST CHOICE FOR LIVED-IN SKIN By Terry Gelee de Rose Intensive Multi-Active Moisturizer ($93), Eve Lom TLC Radiance Cream ($72), Aesop Perfect Facial Hydrating Cream ($120), L'Oreal Paris Youth Code Day/Night Cream Moisturizer ($25), Boots No7 Protect & Perfect Night Cream ($21), RoC Retinol Correxion Sensitive Night Cream ($21)

# 5. A BROAD-SPECTRUM SUNSCREEN WITH SPF 30+

For work and everyday running around, a moisturizer with a broad-spectrum sunscreen in the formula is fine. For longer periods of time outdoors, summer, and beach vacations, you will need to upgrade to a real sunscreen with a broad spectrum UVA/UVB protection of SPF 30+. An oil-free or sheer, nonshiny formula slips easily under makeup and won't look greasy, chalky, or heavy. If your skin is on the dry side, a more moisturizing sunscreen can work solo (without an additional layer of moisturizer) or under makeup.

### BEST CHOICE FOR TROUBLED SKIN

Neutrogena Ultra-Sheer Dry Touch Sunscreen SPF 45 ($8), L'Oreal Paris Sublime Sun Advanced Sunscreen SPF 50 ($11)

### BEST CHOICE FOR LIVED-IN SKIN La Roche Posay Anthelios 50 Daily Anti-Aging Primer with Sunscreen ($40)

# 6. AN EYE CREAM, GEL, OR SERUM

The skin around the eyes is thinner and is the first place to show signs of stress, lack of sleep, age, or genetics. You may notice puffiness, circles, or a dry, tired look, especially when you've had too much alcohol or salt the night before. Some eye discolorations are hereditary. Although you could use your usual face moisturizer under your eyes, a specialized eye treatment offers targeted benefits. Those with peptides, retinol, or algae tighten, and caffeine added as an ingredient deflates puffiness. A big dose of hyaluronic acid fills in lines and crow's-feet so eyes look wide awake.

### BEST CHOICE FOR PUFFY EYES June Jacobs Revitalizing Eye Gel ($96), MAC Fast Response Eye Cream ($30), 100% Pure Coffee Bean Caffeine Eye Cream ($18)

### BEST CHOICE FOR CIRCLES AND SAGGY EYES Olay Regenerist Eye Lifting Serum ($20), La Mer The Eye Balm Intense ($125), Neutrogena Ageless Intensives Anti-Wrinkle Deep Wrinkle Eye Cream ($20), L'Oreal Paris Revitalift Triple Power Eye Treatment ($20)

# 7. AN INTENSIVE SERUM

Yes, it's another step, but serums have higher concentrations of active ingredients and smaller molecules so they penetrate deeper into the skin. Choose one that intensifies or enhances the corrective ingredients in your moisturizer. Selecting one from the same brand makes this easy to do and foolproof. Most lived-in skin benefits from a serum added to their night routine. Those with troubled skin may want to skip this step with the exception of red, irritated, unblemished skin,

which can improve with calming botanical extracts like licorice and marshmallow, soothing green tea extract, and B vitamins.

**BEST CHOICE FOR TROUBLED SKIN** Boots Botanics Ultra Calm Skin Relief Serum ($16), Olay Regenerist Daily Regenerating Serum ($22), L'Oreal Paris Youth Code Regenerating Skincare Serum Intense Daily Treatment ($23)

**BEST CHOICE FOR LIVED-IN SKIN** Eve Lom Intensive Hydration Serum ($95), Boots No7 Protect & Perfect Intense Beauty Serum ($24), RoC Retinol Correxion Deep Wrinkle Serum ($21)

# 8. A SKIN-BOOSTING FACIAL MASK

This special category of detox skin care may be a once or twice a week routine for you. The kind you select depends on your skin needs. Some masks are radiance boosters and contain some combo of vitamins, minerals, retinol, and AHA acids that brighten and restore a glow when you're tired or looking stressed. Others clarify skin prone to blemishes; deep clean pores; and dry up excess oil with a base of clay, mud, or sulfur. And still other masks ramp up moisture so your face looks firmer and skin seems dewier.

**BEST CHOICE FOR TROUBLED SKIN**
Erno Laszlo Anti-Blemish Beta Mask ($50), Tata Harper Resurfacing Mask ($55), Bliss That's Incredi-Peel! ($49), Chantecaille Detox Clay Mask ($78), Freeman Facial Clay Mask with Avocado and Oatmeal ($4), Kiss My Face Potent & Pure Pore Deep Cleansing Mask ($14)

**BEST CHOICE FOR LIVED-IN SKIN** Clarins Super Restorative Replenishing Comfort Mask ($62), Darphin Youthful Radiance Camellia Mask ($70), Freeman Feeling Beautiful Facial Enzyme Mask with Pineapple ($4), Avene Soothing Moisture Mask ($24), Burt's Bees Intense Hydration Treatment Mask ($18)

# 9. BODY SCRUB/WASH/CREAM

You need a moisturizing bodywash and post-shower/bath body cream plus an exfoliating scrub. Pros always say to switch to lukewarm water, but c'mon, who does that?! So just don't linger, and use a moisturizing bodywash, not deodorant or antibacterial soap. Towel-blot and apply a moisturizer while skin is still damp. Use a moisturizing bodywash with buffing beads or just add bath-scrub gloves (available at drugstores) to your daily routine. You'll avoid flakes on the inside of tights and black clothes!

**BEST CHOICE FOR SCRUBS** June Jacobs Lemon Sugar Body Polish ($48), Ahava Deadsea Salt Softening Butter Salt Scrub ($24)

**BEST CHOICE FOR BODYWASH** Olay Ultra Moisture Bodywash with Shea Butter ($6), Olay Total Effects 7-in-1 Exfoliate & Replenish Bodywash ($7)

**BEST CHOICE FOR BODY LOTION/ CREAM** CeraVe Moisturizing Lotion ($12), Kai Body Butter ($52)

# 10. A GRADUAL SELF-TANNER/MOISTURIZER AND A TOTAL SELF-TANNER

Every light to medium skin tone looks better with the daily glow of a moisturizer with built-in gradual self-tanner. For an immediate skin boost—for going bare for vacations, dates, and big evenings—nothing beats the speed of a full-strength self-tanner. It instantly hides discolorations, slims your body, and gives your skin a more even look.

**BEST CHOICE** St. Tropez Gradual Everyday Tan for the Body ($30), St. Tropez Self-Tan Mousse ($32), L'Oreal Paris Sublime Bronze Self-Tanning Towelettes for Body( $10), Jergens Natural Glow Foaming Daily Moisturizer for the Face ($10).

# FACE

Every Successful Girl can have beautiful skin if she is strategic about daily care and long-term goals. My professional spa secrets and DIY tips will get you there.

## CLEANSER

This liquid, gel, foam, or cream removes daily dirt and excess oil that clog pores and dull your skin's appearance. Most skins do not appreciate being overly cleansed, so avoid stripping the skin of all its natural oils. Straight-up soap, which does just that, will work against you. A fancy cleanser is not necessary, just the formula that's right for your needs. FYI, a cleanser does not double as a serious makeup remover. Use a separate product to take off full foundation, blush, bronzer, sunscreen, and eye makeup thoroughly.

### If your skin is troubled.

Choose a clear gel or foam cleanser that's fragrance free. Look for the antibacterial ingredient benzoyl peroxide to help prevent new breakouts or anti-inflammatory ingredients like salicylic acid, green tea, feverfew, and chamomile to calm redness and give your skin a brighter cleaner

look. For mature troubled skin, look for a combo of salicylic acid and a proven de-aging AHA (alpha hydroxyl acid) like glycolic acid to tackle lines and acne.

**GRETTA'S SPA SECRET:** Use flat cotton disks or quilted cotton squares (available at the drugstore) instead of your fingers to gently wash your face like spa pros do. Moisten the pad with water, add cleanser, and massage lightly in a circular motion. Don't scrub. Be gentle, and never substitute a washcloth for cotton pads. Washcloths are far too abrasive. This technique removes all surface debris and gives you a spa-fresh feeling.

### If your skin is lived-in.

Choose a milky, foam, or cream cleanser to counteract dryness, soften, and hydrate. Look for nourishing hydrating ingredients like soy (for amino acid proteins), shea butter, or borage seed oil.

**GRETTA'S SPA SECRET:** Every celeb goes to a salon, day spa, or dermatologist for a deep-cleansing facial or light glycolic acid peel before a photo shoot. If you have a major event—a party, wedding, job interview, date—this is the time for you to splurge on one too. It takes your at-home cleansing and exfoliating to the next level.

## EXFOLIATION

The renewal cycle of skin cells slows with age, but even in your twenties and thirties, dead cells on the surface can dull your complexion and emphasize blackheads and flakiness. Unless you're assertive (but gentle!) about polishing these dead cells away, you'll never have successful skin. You have four choices. The first is to combine any liquid, gel, foam, or cream cleanser with the extra-exfoliating push of a sonic brush or even a soft manual face brush. A second option is an

exfoliating cleanser with built-in cleansing grains or skin-polishing microbeads that speed up cell turnover. Both combine two steps in one. An exfoliating mask that uses fruit enzymes to chemically dissolve dead cells once or twice a week and at-home DIY acid peels with BHA (beta hydroxy acid, such as salicylic acid) or a combo of AHA and BHA on presaturated pads also effectively boost exfoliation. Whichever routine you choose, get rid of the top layer of extra junk so treatment serums and creams can penetrate and do their work. Exfoliation also provides an instant circulation boost so skin looks instantly brighter, smoother, and makeup glides on.

### If your skin is troubled.

Stay away from textured exfoliating scrubs and abrasive face polishes. Instead, look for exfoliating masks and peels to remove sluggish dead cells, oil, and dirt trapped in pores. If you use a sonic brush, get one with a soft-sensitive head. Leave the extraction of clogs and blemishes to skin spa aestheticians or a dermatologist. They know how to deep clean without the risk of marks or infection. Do not pick or squeeze yourself. Your dermatologist may prescribe Retin-A as a treatment for its exfoliating effect on skin and successful treatment of acne (and sun damage!).

**GRETTA'S SPA SECRET:** Do a salonlike facial steaming at home followed by a mask with clay, salicylic acid, or sulfur, or a peel-away mask that actually reveals all the crud you've pulled out of your skin! To do a steam, remove your makeup and cleanse your face. Fill a clean bathroom sink with hot water and place your face over the bowl so the steam reaches your pores. Drape a towel over your head to form a tent, and stay that way for seven to ten minutes. Drain the sink and rinse your face with cool water.

### If your skin is lived-in.

Put more effort into exfoliation to hit the bull's-eye. Sonic brushes, peels, and masks should all be part of your daily/weekly routine. Be gentle but persistent, since the rosy glow you get from exfoliating is cumulative and remains only with regular upkeep.

**GRETTA'S SPA SECRET:** More is more. Every day, exfoliate in the a.m. with a physical exfoliant like a sonic brush (used with your cleanser) or a facial cleanser with polishing grains or beads. Then continue the process at night with a serum or cream that has regenerating vitamins, collagen- boosting retinol, or major doses of super-hydrating hyaluronic acid to restore a dewy, plump texture.

# MOISTURIZER

Every girl wants to find the one perfect cream. That's a lot of responsibility for one product to deliver, but a 2-in-1 is ideal for minimalists and speedy types. Like many women, I hate using a separate sunscreen during the day and look for moisturizers with broad-spectrum sunscreen built into the formula. If you prefer a morning/night do-it-all cream, be sure you are getting the right ingredients to supply your skin with a continuous infusion of moisture and de-aging benefits too. Even in your twenties, sun damage can already be causing the collagen support system of your skin to break down, even if you can't see it… yet. You may opt to use a daily moisturizer with built in broad-spectrum sunscreen and a more intense cream at night when your skin is makeup free.

No matter what your age, look for moisturizers with proven ingredients. You want humectants like hyaluronic acid, glycerin, butylene glycol, propylene glycol, lactic acid, and urea that pull water from the air straight to your skin and hold it there. Retinol, of course, is the one FDA-approved ingredient that boosts and rebuilds the skin's underlying collagen fiber network. This gives your skin a firm look. You want antioxidants like soy, grapeseed extract, and vitamins A, C, and E to prevent discoloration created by free radicals. Free radicals are molecules produced by sun exposure, pollution, and the environment that threaten skin with pigment changes like brown spots. You can trust AHAs like glycolic, lactic, malic, citric, and tartaric acid to speed up exfoliation so fresh cells rise to the top, and emollients like shea butter and plant oils to lubricate and strengthen the skin's outer barrier for better moisture retention.

Four other ingredients are also frequently listed on moisturizers. Here they are and what they do: niacinamide (vitamin B3) helps fade discolorations; ceramides improve the barrier function of your skin to prevent water loss; peptides are long chains of amino acids, and they can help restore a thicker, firmer texture; and copper peptides help mature or sun-damaged skin regenerate. Serums are often sold as companion products to moisturizers and are meant to be layered under them. They are super-concentrated and contain higher percentages of active ingredients to supplement your cream, but they don't do the job of hydrating, so don't think this is an either/or situation.

## If your skin is troubled.

Choose an oil-free gel-cream or lightweight lotion that hydrates without heavy emollients or potential skin irritants. Look for simple products free of parabens, sulfates, synthetic dyes, and petrochemicals. But don't skip moisturizer. Your skin can be oily and dehydrated.

**GRETTA'S SPA SECRET:** Look for moisturizer in a tube or pump bottle for hygiene purposes. You don't want to double dip, especially if your skin has problems to begin with. If you select an open-mouth jar, use a fresh cotton swab to dip—not your fingers, which can contaminate the product. Apply moisturizer to gently blotted, still-damp skin or mist your face with water before applying moisturizer for better absorption.

## If your skin is lived-in.

Look for proven (see full list under "Moisturizer") de-agers like antioxidant vitamins C and E, retinol, AHAs and hyaluronic acid, and glycerin to attract moisture and lock it in. You want a cream that is rich but not heavy or greasy. Layer a compatible serum under your day or night cream to increase your skincare benefits.

**GRETTA'S SPA SECRET:** Use your moisturizer as a hydrating mask. Simply apply a thicker layer for an intensive boost, and let it sink in for five to ten minutes before blotting off the excess and applying makeup.

# EYE CREAM

This is one extra that is crucial if your eye area tends to look puffy, fatigued, deeply circled, red, or tired. Keep a chilled eye gel or cream in the fridge, since the cold helps reduces swelling more quickly. Look for active ingredients that deflate, like caffeine and vitamin K, soothing ingredients like cucumber extract and green tea, and firming ingredients like horse chestnut, peptides, and algae extract. Yes, models sometimes do use hemorrhoid cream with the ingredient phenylephrine, and it does work, but why use it when you have better options ?!

**GRETTA'S SPA SECRET:** You can also dampen disposable cotton pads (they come in quilted disks and squares at the drugstore) with water or witch hazel and keep them in the fridge or freezer to apply in the morning. They counteract a puffy face or swollen eyes!

Every girl wants to find the one perfect cream.

# BODY

Displaying well-cared-for skin from the neck down is important now that sleeveless dresses, low, bare necklines, and bare legs are part of the Successful Girl's year-round style. Always use your facial moisturizer and treatments on your neck and chest too, but pay attention to the rest with a planned strategy so you can show skin 24/7 without a thought.

## Body exfoliation.

Make buffing dead cells from your arms, legs, and back a 365-days-a-year routine. Dead cells also pile up on the surface here, giving your skin a flaky, dull, ashy, scaly look. If you're a shower girl, use a daily exfoliating bodywash with polishing beads or a bodywash with textured scrub gloves (or a wash cloth) to enhance slough-ing. The advantage to gloves and washcloths is, unlike brushes, they can be easily sterilized in boiling water or a microwave. Bath girls or shower girls wanting a more intense polish can do a sugar- or salt-based scrub in the tub once or twice a week.

**GRETTA'S SPA SECRET:** Make your own scrub by adding a couple of tablespoons of grapeseed, jojoba, rose, safflower, or almond oil from the health-food store to a quarter cup of sea salt or sugar (preferable if you have sensitive skin). Add a drop or two of some sensual scented oil or perfume, and you have a $100 spa scrub at home for a lot less. For super-dry skin, add shea butter to the mix—it's the Rolls-Royce of emollients. You'll get a higher con-centration of active ingredients this way and can save and store what-ever is left over till next time. Just keep it away from heat and humidity.

## Feet.

Keep your feet pedicure-ready and bare-able 24/7. Like clothes, open peep-toes, strappy cage booties, and, in some parts of the country, sandals are a year-round style option. Maintaining feet weekly makes this easy and can be part of a bath soak/scrub. Use a pumice or emery board on dry feet to smooth calluses and rough spots before stepping into the tub. Soak in the tub and massage the same oil/salt/sugar mix over your feet too.

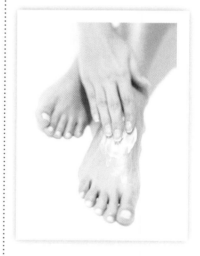

**GRETTA'S SPA SECRET:** Before bed, apply a rich foot cream or any thick, leftover face cream to clean, dry feet straight out of the tub or shower. Really slather it on in a coat, like frosting a cupcake. Slip your feet into plastic sandwich bags, and then slip your feet into socks. Sleep in them overnight for silky dogs in the morning.

## Hands & cuticles.

Your hands and nails should always be groomed and fresh, even if they're just buffed minus polish. Every day, apply a hand cream with SPF 30 and de-agers like AHAs. Keep reapplying frequently throughout the day. At night, apply a layer of natural oil—olive or almond work fine—under your hand cream.

**GRETTA'S SPA SECRET:** Double up your plastic-bag-and-sock-treatment for your hands as well. Use the same technique, but sub a rich hand cream or leftover face cream for foot cream and keep them on overnight too!

## Nails.

I'm a spa junkie, so I find a salon/spa manicure/pedicure one of the best ways to relax and de-stress. Groomed nails send a positive instant message that goes beyond style. Do them yourself or go to a salon—your choice—but keep them polished and flawless. We talk with our hands, reference and gesture with them, so there's a high visibility factor here. Nail care is one of the least expensive ways to look fresh and classy. The old rules about neutral colors for work have pretty much gone, with the exception of women in the food and medical field, who usually opt for sheer, natural, nude tones that create a clean image. The entire neutral category, FYI, now goes from pale to dark, cool gray to warm brown, and includes creams, shimmer, metallics, or sparkle.

Gel manicures have cut down on maintenance since they last two solid weeks without a chip and are available in at-home kits or at the salon. Successful Girls stay true to their style and know when a trendy color is too good to miss or just too much—and in that case she just might do it on toes just for the fun of it.

## Gradual self-tanner.

Every Successful Girl with skin-tone concerns (especially those with light to medium skin tones) benefits from a daily moisturizer/gradual self-tanner to give her skin an even, subtle tint. This builds over several days with continued use. You control the degree of color. Apply it every day to build up skin tone, or every other day to keep the look minimal. If you have discolorations like blotchy or pigmented areas from sun damage or sensitivity issues, under-eye circles, broken capillaries, or veins on your legs or your complexion looks ashy, tired, or sallow, this is the solution. You're always ready for that deep-V neckline or halter or a mini without pantyhose. Being able to show well-cared-for skin at a moment's notice expands your style confidence.

**GRETTA'S SPA SECRET:** Use a gradual face tanner/moisturizer as a glowing base for makeup. It blurs discolorations and makes using minimal makeup like a BB cream easy to wear.

## Full-strength self-tanner.

Real self-tanner gives more of an immediate color boost—the kind you'd get from a week-away tropical vacation. I'm a big fan of self-tanner as a base for every makeover I do. It slims and upgrades skin that's uneven and gives arms and legs a slimmer overall appearance. It immediately enables you to show more skin comfortably. I like St. Tropez Self Tan Bronzing Mousse and L'Oreal Paris Sublime Bronze Self-Tanning Towelettes for Body. A dry oil misted on shins and arms can give your self-tanned bronzed skin tone a subtle sheen for evening dates and events.

**GRETTA'S SPA SECRET:** Get a spray tan at a day spa for the most even and quickest tan that will last a week. There's no mess, and the technician gets spots you'd miss for the most authentic look. Wear old black clothes and leave modesty at the door. Exfoliate before arriving at the salon. If you want to replicate the look at home, choose a spray with a 360-degree nozzle to make getting hard-to-reach areas like your back and booty easy. Use the spray in the shower so cleanup is easy.

> Being able to show well-cared-for skin at a moment's notice expands your style confidence.

# HAIR REMOVAL FACE AND BODY

What you consider excess face and body hair is a very personal decision. There are no rules, but once you opt for removal, your skin sensitivity and the density of the hair in the area concerned are the key factors. Head-to-toe hair removal has grown as pro bikini waxing and brow maintenance routines jumped from celebs only to everyday women. It also prompted a demand for more precise and painless procedures, as well as DIY tools and kits. Whether you go to a salon or day spa or trust your own skill, hair removal is not a big deal anymore.

Your pro-removal options include threading, waxing, laser, and electrolysis. Your at-home DIY choices include shaving, depilatories, waxing, and the new at-home lasers.

Let's start with brow shaping because, in my opinion, the more brow you have, the better—women tend to overdo hair removal here. The goal is to achieve the best possible shape to frame and enhance your eyes. Full, lush, well-shaped brows look youthful and give every face definition. The grooming of your brows contributes to the success of your look in a big way. Consider brow care as more about growing brows in and maintaining shape. If your brows are thin or overplucked, you might consider brow regrowth treatments. These are available by prescription at your dermatologist (like the drug Latisse) and over-the-counter (like RapidLash Eyelash and Eyebrow Renewal Serum). They do work, but give them six to eight weeks.

For the rest of your face, at-home pretreated wax strips are frankly easy to do. They give great results for the mustache area above your upper lip, chin, and sideburns. Be sure to do a patch test first on a low-visibility area like the nape of your neck. Be prepared for a slight tingle. I like the Sally Hansen Hair Remover Wax Strip Kits from the drugstore for fine to coarse facial hair. They're a cinch even for a first-time waxing novice. Some women with a few fine dark hairs above the lip prefer to bleach using a facial hair product designed for that area.

**GRETTA'S SPA SECRET:** You can reuse the same wax strip on multiple spots during the same hair removal session. For example, the same strip can be used on your upper lip and then reused on the chin or sideburn area, like a lint roller.

Legs are a great DIY area for at-home removal. Most women find waxing strips give a clean, silky result, while others don't mind the routine of shaving or chemical depilatories. The biggest issue is which "down-under" hair removal method to select, especially if you have coarse bikini hair. I've tried every single procedure from shaving to waxing, and I now laser my bikini line twice a year because I want the longest-lasting treatment. Laser removal is a pricey investment, so know that hair regrowth is finer and slower, but any claims for quick, totally hair-free results are overstated. At least that's my experience! After four years, I'm still at it but still holding out hope that the payoff will come with time.

# HOW TO DO SUCCESSFUL MAKEUP

TIME TO SYNC UP YOUR BEAUTY AND STYLE. THE REST OF THIS CHAPTER IS ALL ABOUT THE ICING ON THE STYLE CAKE. IF YOU GO BACK TO YOUR INSPIRATION BOARD, YOU'LL NOTICE THAT THE LOOKS YOU LOVE HAVE A SEAMLESS HEAD-TO-TOE FLOW. EACH STYLE—WEEKEND, GIRLY, SOPHISTICATED, AND SEXY—IS MOST SUCCESSFUL WHEN THE HAIR AND MAKEUP WORK WITH THE CLOTHES AND COMPLEMENT ONE ANOTHER IN A BALANCED WAY. WE'RE STARTING WITH MAKEUP. NO MATTER WHAT YOUR FACIAL FEATURES OR SKIN TONE, THERE ARE TEN PRODUCTS THAT BELONG IN EVERY SUCCESSFUL GIRL'S KIT. THEY'RE NOT SUPER-GLITZY EXTRAS OR TRENDS-OF-THE-MINUTE FADS, JUST THE HARD WORKING ESSENTIALS THAT PULL YOUR LOOKS TOGETHER FAST AND GET YOU THROUGH 24/7.

*Every makeup pro who works on celebs suggests applying makeup in natural light near a window.*

# THE GOTTA-HAVES

## This is your successful makeup kit

## 1. A CONCEALER

A creamy, matte, opaque concealer will cover blemishes and undereye circles. Brush-on pen-types with light reflectors are good for the delicate, dry, inner eye corners, but they should have enough coverage ability too.

**BEST CHOICE FOR STICK OR CREAM**
Cle de Peau Beaute Concealer ($70), Lancôme Effacernes Waterproof Under-Eye Concealer ($30), L'Oreal Paris True Match Super-blendable Crayon Concealer ($9)

**BEST CHOICE FOR PEN BRUSH-ON**
Trish McEvoy Flawless Concealer ($38), Neutrogena Healthy Skin Brightening Eye Perfector ($13)

## 2. A BB CREAM

This category of light, ramped-up, tinted moisturizers has more intense ingredients and technology. They provide subtle coverage, a tinted glow, and problem-solving options ranging from de-aging to blemish-clearing. Since they actually are hybrid skincare/makeup products, select them with the same goals as a moisturizer or cleanser. Some come in one adjusts-to-fit-all-skin-tones shade, while others are available in a range of skin tone shades. The finishes vary from dewy to matte, and the degree of sun protection ranges from a broad-spectrum SPF 15 to 45. They work alone and make perfect primers as a skin base for foundation with more coverage. If you prefer makeup with full coverage, an untinted primer rather than BB cream is all you need for the extra slip-on application and long all-day wear.

**BEST CHOICE FOR TROUBLED SKIN**
Smashbox Camera Ready BB Cream SPF 35 ($39), Stila All Day 10-in-1 HD Beauty Balm with Broad Spectrum SPF 30 ($38), Too Faced Air Buffed BB Creme Complete Coverage Makeup Broad Spectrum Sunscreen SPF 20 ($39)

**BEST CHOICE FOR LIVED-IN SKIN** Clinique Age Defense BB Cream Broad Spectrum SPF 30 ($37), Bobbi Brown BB Cream Broad Spectrum SPF 30 ($42), L'Oreal Paris Age Perfect BB

Cream SPF 20 ($17)

# 3. A REAL FOUNDATION

While BB creams are great for a natural look or as a primer, you still need a skin-perfecting base with medium to full coverage, especially if you have blemish-prone or blotchy skin. It can be a texture you're comfortable with, including a compact gel-cream, liquid, or cream. Choose a shade that enhances, not matches, your natural skin tone. Women often go too light in shade selection and end up looking masky and made-up. A shade warmer/richer/deeper than you think is often the best one. Look for buildable formulas that allow you to layer more coverage on discolored or blemished areas. I'm a fan of creams and spray foundation, which I sometimes apply with a big, fluffy brush. Oil-free formulas are good for troubled skin, while lived-in skin can benefit from more hydration.

## BEST CHOICE FOR TROUBLED SKIN
Smashbox Studio Skin 15-Hour Wear Foundation ($42), Too Faced Air-Buffed BB Creme Complete

Coverage Makeup ($39), Chantecaille Future Skin Foundation ($72), Neutrogena SkinClearing Oil-Free Makeup ($14)

## BEST CHOICE FOR LIVED-IN SKIN
Dior Beauty Airflash Spray Foundation ($62), Armani Designer Shaping Cream Foundation SPF 20 ($65), Becca Radiant Skin Satin Finish Foundation ($42), Revlon Nearly Naked Makeup SPF 20 ($10), Revlon ColorStay Whipped Creme Makeup ($14), L'Oreal Paris Visible Lift Repair Absolute Rapid Age Reversing Makeup ($15), L'Oreal Paris True Match Lumi Healthy Luminous Makeup SPF 20 ($13)

## 4. SHEER BLUSH

Stick to ultrasheer blush in a rose, pink, or golden apricot shade. These work with every skin tone and give your skin a boost without looking painted on. Any other color or a matte opaque texture looks too strong or clownish. Products that tint cheeks and lips with soft, sheer, creamy color like NARS Multiple and Stila Convertible Color are my go-tos.

**BEST CHOICE FOR CREAM** NARS The Multiple ($39), Stila Convertible Color ($25), Armani Sheer Blush ($44), By Terry Velvet Cream Blush ($44), Maybelline Dream Bouncy Blush ($8), L'Oreal Paris Visible Lift Color Lift Blush ($13)

**BEST CHOICE FOR POWDER**
Maybelline Fit Me! Blush ($6)

## 5. TWEEZERS & BROW MAKEUP

You need slant-tipped tweezers for shaping and a pointy-tipped-tweezers to grab stubble and ingrown hairs. To fill, extend, and amplify shape, opt for a fine-tipped automatic pencil, which allows you to sketch in tiny hairlike strokes, and a powder brow kit that comes with a wax primer and a duo or trio of natural soft shades. Minimalists or women with naturally lush brows may just use a tinted brow gel for a hint of color and control.

**BEST CHOICE TWEEZER** Tweezerman Slant Tweezer ($25), Tweezerman Point Tip Tweezer ($23)

**BEST CHOICE BROW MAKEUP**
Smashbox Brow Tech ($25), DiorShow Brow Styler ($29), Trish McEvoy Precision Brow Shaper ($28), Sephora Eyebrow Editor Complete Brow Kit ($19)

## 6. LIP SHINE

Any kind of formula—lipstick, lip crayon, gloss, stain, or tinted balm—that leaves your lips looking moist and fresh is best. It can be creamy, shimmery, or sheer, but skip anything matte—it may be trendy, but it's aging for everyone.

**BEST CHOICE** Tarte LipSurgence Lip Tint ($24), Yves Saint Laurent Rouge Pur Couture Vernis A Lèvres Glossy Stain ($34), Fresh Sugar Tinted Lip Treatment ($22.50), Clinique Chubby Stick Intense Moisturizing Lip Colour Balm ($16), Stila Color Balm Lipstick ($22), Revlon ColorBurst Lip Butter ($7), L'Oreal Colour Riche Caresse Wet Shine Stain ($10)

## 7. A BRONZING POWDER

A powder in a compact with a semisatin finish gives the most authentic glow. Stay away from matte bronzers, shimmery/shiny metallic bronzers, and liquid or cream bronzers since they can be hard to control. Choose a shade one or two times deeper than your skin tone or a multicolor bronzer that includes a range of shades to swirl together.

**BEST CHOICE** Illamasqua Bronzing Duo ($34), Diorskin Nude Tan Healthy Glow Enhancing Powder ($55), Physicians Formula Bronze Booster Glow Boosting Pressed Bronzer ($15), Iman Sheer Finish Bronzing Powder ($16)

## 8. EYE LINER PENCIL

You really only need a black, brown, or charcoal classic long-wear pencil, although there are so many options now from felt-tip pens to brush on creams and liquids that playing with other formulas is irresistible. For a cat-eye look, a felt-tip pen or a gel liquid are great and easy.

**BEST CHOICE** Urban Decay 24/7 Glide-On Eye Pencil ($19), Maybelline Unstoppable Eyeliner ($6)

# 9. NEUTRAL EYESHADOWS

A neutral palette in warm or cool tones that includes a range of light to dark shades for your lids and crease contour and to use as liner (or directly over pencil liner to soften and reinforce it) in a satin or matte finishes is all you need. These shades can go to work or out for the evening and layer up to intensify the effect or get a smoky look fast. They work for every eye and hair color or skin-tone.

**BEST CHOICE** Urban Decay Naked 2 Palette ($50), Stila in the Know Eye Shadow Palette ($39), Tarte Call of The Wild Amazonian Clay 8-Shadow Collector's Palette ($36), Lorac Unzipped ($40), Smashbox Photo Op Eye Enhancing Palette ($39), Maybelline ExpertWear Quad Eyeshadow ($5), Maybelline EyeStudio Eyeshadow Quad ($10), Wet n Wild Color Icon Collection Eyeshadow Trio ($3)

# 10. AN EYELASH CURLER & BLACK MASCARA

You need to curl your lashes first no matter what mascara your choose. Look for a traditional, full-size, metal lash-curler with silicone sponge cushion in a wide-elongated arc to prevent the crimping that low-cost U-shaped curlers give. Skip gimmicky, heated, mini, or plastic curlers. The Successful Girl needs only black mascara no matter what brand or formula. It's really all about the brush, and I look for a thick, dense shape for a lush lay-down of color but also for bristles that separate. For extra drama, I like adding fake lashes (for dating, evenings out). Nothing beats the instant glamour and the way they make your eyes stand out.

**BEST CHOICE CURLER** Shu Uemura Eye Lash Curler ($20), Le Metier de Beaute Curler ($18)

**BEST CHOICE MASCARA** L'Oreal Paris Voluminous Mascara ($9), Dior Diorshow Black Out Mascara ($25)

**BEST CHOICE FAKE LASHES** Ardell Fashion Lashes ($4), Andrea Modlash ($4)

# GRETTA'S 24/7 MAKEUP PLAN

My basic everyday makeup strategy gives every Successful Girl a head start for a busy multitasking day. Be sure you use a mirror that is big enough—your compact or rearview car mirror are not. If you need a magnifying mirror for accurate application and blending, use one. Large, free-standing ovals that swivel from regular to magnifying in plain and lighted versions are available for $25 and up from Revlon, Conair, and other brands at sites like walmart.com and bedbathandbeyond.com. They're helpful for detail work.

## 1. Keep your makeup ready, your lighting right.

Organize your products so the ones you use daily are handy for immediate application. The Container Store (containerstore.com) has a huge selection of baskets, as well as lacquered and lucite boxes, that look attractive on a vanity. Keep all makeup fresh (no grimy compacts, unsharpened pencils, messy brushes, or sponges with leftover makeup residue) and ready to work. Every makeup pro who works on celebs suggests applying makeup in natural light near a window, but realistically most women do their makeup in a bathroom, vanity alcove near the bathroom, or their bedroom. What you want to avoid is fluorescent lighting, which can distort makeup colors and make achieving a natural look difficult. Changing the bulbs to full-spectrum light instead is a simple, inexpensive solution.

## 2. Apply skin care to a clean face.

Cleanse your face just before applying your daily treatment/moisturizer. Your skin will be warm and glowing from the circulation boost and most receptive to skin care. Remember to moisturize your neck too and any part of your chest that will be visible. Apply your non-greasy day eye cream under the eye and in the inner corner where skin is thinnest and driest. Let all skin treatment sink in for two or three minutes so you start makeup with a healthy, glowing surface. Blot off excess.

## 3. Use a primer or BB cream as a primer.

Either product will keep your makeup looking clean and just-applied for a full-packed day. You don't have time to redo during a multitasking day or a long day into evening, and a BB or primer works as the first layer of your makeup "sandwich." You'd never paint a wall without a base coat of primer—same thing.

## 4. Apply foundation for extra color and camouflage.

I prefer to do my basic face makeup before eyes. Even skin provides a more inspiring "canvas" to work on. If BB cream provides enough color and camouflage for you and/or you prefer a minimal natural look, skip this step. Otherwise apply foundation (see above for details) from center of face outwards in a sheer layer, feathering the coverage toward the edges of your face and hairline. Make sure the makeup melts seamlessly into the borders of your face around jaw, hairline, and ears. Nothing is worse than when a woman turns profile and you can see where the makeup stops and starts. Use fingers, a foundation brush, or a makeup sponge to apply and blend, whichever makes you most comfortable. If your skin is clear and needs minimal correction, a single sheer pass with foundation is enough. For troubled skin, layer more makeup where needed to help minimize blemishes, age spots, and redness. You want to build coverage slowly, not apply a thick, heavy coat. The goal is to blur any imperfections for a natural more even look, not to create totally fake, flawless skin. (Ads are always retouched, so don't aim for that kind of perfection.)

## 5. Use concealer or your foundation to address discolorations.

To minimize blue, purple, or brownish discolorations under the eyes and at the inner eye corner near the nose, or blemishes and redness around the nose, use a creamy concealer. A kit with multiple shades allows you to customize coverage for multiple discolorations. You can also use your foundation as a concealer, adding additional layers with a clean, flat eye brush.

## 6. Contour eyes for shape.

Here's where your neutral eye kit plays up your eyes. Apply a pale shadow as a base on upper lids, from lash line to brows. Then layer a medium shade right over it, lashes to just above the crease to add depth. You can use the very darkest shadow (a charcoal or mahogany, for example) as a soft liner, brushing it close to the lashes, or go on to step 7 for a stronger look.

## 7. Line with pencil for extra definition.

Apply your black, brown, or charcoal liner pencil at the upper lash line, using short back-and-forth strokes to get the color between the lashes at the roots. Go back over the pencil line with matching dark black, dark brown, or charcoal shadow using a firm-eye angle brush. This gets rid of any waxy pencil look, reduces smearing, and makes liner last.

## 8. Use an eyelash curler and black mascara to wake up eyes.

Curling lashes prior to mascara swoops your lashes up so you look rested and alert. Press and hold for three seconds close to the roots of the lashes. Follow with two or three coats of black long-wear mascara. If your lids are oily or your eyes tear, choose a waterproof formula. For evening, add fake lashes.

## 9. Fill in and extend brows to frame your eyes.

Go a little lighter in shade than your actual brow color, since brow makeup always appears deeper once applied. Keep the look natural, and use a light touch. Stroke pencil on in upward, feathery, hairline strokes solo to fill sparse spots and stretch the brow tail out. If you use powder brow makeup, stroke color on in the direction of hair growth. To re-create brows at overplucked inner corners or the outer half where hair is missing, pencil or use a wax base before adding powder so color clings in place.

## 10. Apply blush or bronzer before lips.

You just need a hint to warm up the skin. You want a super-sheer flush or glow here, not an obvious look. Blend your cream or powder blush on top of the cheekbones, starting just under the pupil of your eyes (as you look straight ahead ) and up. If you prefer a sunny look, sweep bronzer on the broad, flat planes of your face— cheekbones, hairline, jawline, down center of neck—not on your nose!

## 11. Enhance lips with color.

I'm not a big believer in lip liner—it's an option, not a must-do. Every Successful Girl looks great with an enhanced natural lip color. Your best natural is not beige—it should be richer, darker, or more intense than your natural lip color by a shade or two. Depending on your individual coloring, it may be a plummy, rosy, pinky, or mauvey neutral. And for Successful Girls who always feel their best in a red lip, do it! Just keep the texture light and fresh.

# IF YOU'RE A
# Weekend Girl

The Weekend Girl prefers an easy, sheer look like Jodie Foster, Jennifer Aniston, Jennifer Garner, or Halle Berry.

**FOR EVERYDAY:** She might stick to a BB cream, a 2-in-1 lip/cheek color like Nars Multiple stick or Stila Convertible cream for cheeks and lips, a sweep of warm nude shadow, mascara, and a tinted brow gel.

**TO GLAM IT UP:** She'll add a golden/peachy highlighter on cheekbones and brow bones, a subtle smudgy liner on eyes, and a glossier lip.

# IF YOU'RE A
# Girly Girl

The Girly Girl loves some color and a hint of sparkle like Zooey Deschanel, Michelle Williams, or Nicole Kidman.

**FOR EVERYDAY:** She might swap a deep navy, hunter, or plum liner for brown or black, do a shimmery neutral shadow on lids, or do a shimmery lipstick in a pinky, rosy color.

**TO GLAM IT UP:** She'll layer a brighter shadow in a real color and add partial fake lashes at the center of the upper lid.

# IF YOU'RE A
# Sophisticated Girl

The Sophisticated Girl likes a defined finished look like Adele, Julianna Margulies, Cate Blanchett, Kate Middleton, or Anne Hathaway.

**FOR EVERYDAY:** She may do a smoky matte eye, a strong, dark liner, and a tawny or red creamy lipstick.

**TO GLAM IT UP:** She'll layer a deep shimmer over that smoky eye, add demi lashes, and refresh her lips with the same lip as day (or do a classic, rich red).

# IF YOU'RE A
# Sexy Girl

The Sexy Girl likes being on trend like Miley Cyrus, Beyoncé, Kim Kardashian, Gwen Stefani, Sofia Vergara, or Olivia Munn.

**FOR EVERYDAY:** She may do a cat-eye with a brush- on liquid or felt-tip liner paired with a nude, red, or whatever-is-hot lip color (from tangerine to pale pink).

**TO GLAM IT UP:** She'll add black or charcoal shadow on lids and rim the inner and outer eye with black.

# HOW TO HAVE SUCCESSFUL HAIR

YOUR HAIR TRULY DEFINES AND REINFORCES YOUR OVERALL STYLE. NOTHING MAKES MORE OF AN IMMEDIATE STATEMENT. IT CAN BE SHORT, MEDIUM, OR LONG—THERE'S NO ONE LENGTH, LOOK, COLOR, OR TEXTURE THAT IS BEST. BUT, YOUR HAIR DOES HAVE TO WORK WITH YOUR FASHION STYLE AND YOUR LIFESTYLE. I'VE LEFT IT TILL LAST BECAUSE THE MORE YOU LEARN ABOUT YOUR STYLE, THE EASIER IT IS TO SELECT THE BEST HAIR FOR YOU.

## Gretta-quette

Some Successful Girls hit on their ideal hair-style early and stay with it, like Rachael Ray, Ellen DeGeneres, Anna Wintour, and Martha Stewart. For some, short hair is faster and more efficient; for others, the same is true of long hair. But we all have moments when we need to try something new. My big hair moment arrived after I gave birth to my son, Kai, and was on maternity leave. I was trying to lose the baby weight and felt in a style rut. Even pros like me sometimes want to put themselves in the hands of other experts! During my early mom phase, I wanted a major change and decided to do it live-on air on the Rachael Ray Show. Stylist Ted Gibson cut twelve inches off to a swingy bob, Jason Backe turned my color to a rich auburn, and makeup artist Scott Barnes gave me his signature Jennifer Lopez bronzy glow. I loved it… but I eventually grew my hair back to its long, signature girly look.

Sometimes one single change or cut can really reinforce your personal style to the point where it becomes a statement, a signature. Think about Michelle Obama cutting her bangs, Anne Hathaway's dramatic short crop, Adele's big bouffant, or Meg Ryan's shag. Some Successful Girls find their best hair look and stick with it, like Martha Stewart or Katie Couric.

Sometimes hair color is the big catalyst, whether you enhance your color or opt for a total change. Successful hair color always has shine and polish, enhances your eyes, and brightens your skin. Some Successful Girls should never color their hair. If it's beautiful and an asset… leave it alone. A consultation with a top colorist or two is essential before you make any color changes. Bring in photos, and be prepared to consider maintenance in terms of finances and routine.

Some hair-care items are what I consider essential to achieving your hair's best look. Included in this list are some splurge items, like the T3 dryer, that I think are worth-it buys for every woman, even if you have to choose low-cost items elsewhere in your routine to make up for it.

# THE GOTTA-HAVES

**This is your successful hair kit**

## 1. A HAIR MASK

A once-or-twice-a-week must for color-treated, chemically-processed. and heat-styled hair, this intensive moisture shot revitalizes hair that is overworked and overexposed to stress. Look for nourishing ingredients like polyphenols, panthenol, jojoba oil, argan extract, sweet almond butter, and shea butter; strengthening, de-aging ingredients like omega-6 fatty acids; and color-preserving ingredients like sunflower extract and UV filters.

**BEST CHOICE** Kerastase Mask Elixir Ultime ($65), Davines Glorifying Anti-Age/Shimmering Pak ($35), Kiehl's Since 1851 Superbly Smoothing Argan Hair Pak ($25), Living Proof Restore Mask Treatment ($42), Phytocitrus Color Protect Radiance Mask ($39), Carol's Daughter Monoi Repairing Hair Mask ($29), Organix Ever Straight Brazilian Keratin Therapy Hydrating Keratin Masque ($7), L'Oreal Paris Advanced Haircare Total Repair 5 Damage Erasing Balm ($7), Garnier Fructis Haircare Sleek & Shine Moroccan Sleek Oil Treatment ($6)

## 2. A SHAMPOO AND CONDITIONER DUO

Select a duo designed to treat as many of your specific hair needs as possible. The selection at every price is endless with new brand extensions popping up on drugstore shelves almost weekly. List your hair type and goals and find the nearest match. Girls with frizzy, dry, color-treated or damaged hair (from excessive chemical or heat exposure ), no matter what their texture (fine to thick) will want a moisturizing shampoo and conditioner. Damaged hair needs protein to rebuild and ceramides to lock in moisture.

**BEST CHOICE FOR COLOR-TREATED HAIR** L'Oreal Paris Kerastase Reflection Bain Chroma Captive ($39) and Lait Richesse Conditioner ($41), L'Oreal Paris Color Vibrancy Nourishing Shampoo ($5) and Conditioner ($5)

**BEST CHOICE FOR FINE, THIN HAIR** Kerastase Bain Volumactive ($39) and Lait Volumcative ($41), Nexxus Hydra Light Weightless Moisture Shampoo ($11) and Conditioner ($16)

**BEST CHOICE FOR DAMAGED HAIR** Kerastase Bain Force Architecte ($39) and Ciment Anti-Usure ($41), Organix Anti-Breakage Keratin Oil Shampoo ($8) and Organix Smooth Hydration Argan Oil & Shea Butter Conditioner ($8)

## 3. A PADDLE BRUSH & STYLING BRUSHES

The Mason Pearson round, flat brush with combo natural boar bristle and synthetic nylon bristles in a bouncy, rubber-padded base lasts forever with care and is my first choice. Medium to long hair will benefit from a full-size, while short hair can opt for the travel size. Round styling brushes that enable you to smooth and straighten sections of hair as you blow-dry are also essential. Choose a size that works for your length. Avoid ceramic brushes that can tear hair, and opt for natural hair bristle rounds instead.

**BEST CHOICE** Mason Pearson Handy Mix Hair Brush and paddle ($120), Marilyn Tuxedo Pro brush ($23)

## 4. A HEAT-PROTECTIVE SPRAY

Very few Successful Girls get away without heat-styling today, but blasting your hair with a blow-dryer and flat iron or curling iron can cause breakage. Prepping hair with a light mist works as a buffer but won't add weight or extra texture to other styling products you apply. Some de-frizz styling products are hybrid heat-stylers and have built-in heat protection, so take advantage of 2-in-1s if they work for your hair goals.

**BEST CHOICE** Oscar Blandi Pronto Dry Styling Heat Protect Spray ($23), John Frieda Frizz Ease Heat Defeat Protective Styling Spray ($6), Tresemme Keratin Smooth Heat Style Spray ($6), John Frieda Frizz-Ease Thermal Protection Serum ($9), Nexxus Heat Protexx Heat Protection Styling Spray ($11)

## 5. AN AMAZING BLOW-DRYER

A pro-quality blow-dryer is an investment you won't regret. Many women complain about the arm-exhausting weight of some dryers and the scorched hair some high-power dryers produce. Select a lightweight but powerful and safe ionic dryer with heat settings and a cool-shot button. Ionic dryers use infrared heat to dry hair from the inside out so it dries faster without overdrying and less frizz. Worth every penny.

**BEST CHOICE** T3 Featherweight Journey Travel Dryer ($130), T3 Featherweight 2 ($200)

## 6. HOT ROLLERS

For speed and volume, hot rollers are ideal. Throw them in while you're doing your makeup to refresh body. The heat makes the curl last longer than Velcro rollers, and the set takes a couple of minutes. The alignment of rollers doesn't have to be perfect. Just grab sections and roll.

**BEST CHOICE** Hot Tools Tourmaline Professional Hairsetter ($36), John Frieda Hairsetter ($40) T3 Voluminous Hot Rollers ($99)

## 7. DRY SHAMPOO

A hot category that extends the life and look of your blow-dry for days and freshens bed-head fast. The newest dry shampoos leave no residue and work as volumizers to build in texture too.

**BEST CHOICE** Oscar Blandi Texture & Volume Spray ($25), L'Oreal Paris Everstyle Energizing Dry Shampoo ($7), John Frieda Luxurious Volume Anytime Volume Refresher ($7)

## 8. PONYTAIL HOLDERS & HAIR ACCESSORIES FOR YOUR HAIR

Hot weather and quick-change days mean you'd better have some hair props on hand. Celebs often rely on hair extensions and pieces for extra volume or length. If you're handy and can add DIY clip-in extensions, clip-in bangs, or even a longer ponytail, HairUWear makes affordable versions in a range of shades for $40 to $100. Simple elastics in a color toned to your hair color, basic black, and neutrals make ponytails chic and modern. Swirl pins sold at drugstores make updos fast and secure but are invisible while in place.

**BEST CHOICE** HairUWear Simply Straight Pony Extension ($40), Goody Thick Ponytail Elastics ($5), Goody Simple Styles Spin Pin ($6)

## 9. A STYLING PRODUCT THAT'S RIGHT FOR YOUR HAIR

Choose a mousse, gel, spray, cream, or balm that delivers the end result you are seeking. This might be more volume, curl, or a straighter look. Styling products are designed to add shape, hold, or definition, or enhance shine. Select one product that multitasks for you.

### BEST CHOICE FOR VOLUME AND SHINE
Oribe Volumista Mist ($38), Alterna Bamboo Volume 48-Hour Sustainable Volume Spray ($24), Redken Guts 10 Volume Spray Foam ($17)

### BEST CHOICE FOR DE-FRIZZ AND SHINE
Josie Maran Argan Oil Hair Serum ($30), Phyto-defrisant Botanical Straightening Balm ($28), L'Oreal Paris Smooth Intense Frizz Taming Serum ($7), Ojon Super Sleek Restorative Blowout perfector ($25)

### BEST CHOICE FOR BODY, CURL, AND SHINE
Ouidad Curl Quencher Hydrafusion Intense Curl Cream ($26), Redken Body Full Carbo-Bodifier Volumizing Foam ($16), John Frieda Frizz-Ease Curl Reviver Styling Mousse ($6)

## 10. A FLAT IRON AND/OR CURLING IRON

These finishing heat-styling tools give hair the polished look you see in magazine editorial pages. They also work for touch-ups to stretch time between blowouts. If your prefer a sleek, straight look, you'll only need the flat iron, but if you want that bouncy, wavy, curly look, a curling iron will get you there. Look for a high-end, ionic flat iron with ceramic plates and temperature control and a curling iron with a one- to one-and-a-half-inch barrel.

**BEST CHOICE** The T3 SinglePass Styling Iron ($160). This is pricey but really guarantees smooth, straight hair without having to repeat sections to achieve a sleek, frizz-free result. Beveled edges let you do flips and waves with the same tool. T3 SinglePass Whirl Professional Styling Wand ($130) is a smart option for curls.

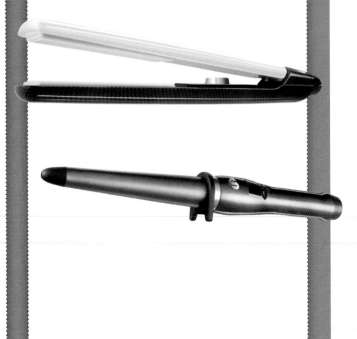

**The right hair look at every length can boost your style.**

# IF YOU LOVE SHORT HAIR

If you love short hair, you may have a true choppy, tousled crop, a boyishly sleek cap of hair, or a layered shag.

### The Weekend Girl

Your style is casual but cool like Halle Berry, Annette Bening, Ellen DeGeneres, Emma Watson, or Rachel Maddow. This is the modern way to do wash-and-wear hair. You need one (if any) style product, never need to worry about how the weather will affect your hair, and the style works for fine to textured hair.

### The Girly Girl

Your style is feminine and you wear makeup as a counterpoint to your short hair like Michelle Williams, Anne Hathaway, Ginnifer Goodwin, or Vanessa Hudgens. It may be waved or crimped, have wisps around the ears and nape, or bangs to flirt under.

### The Sophisticated Girl

Your style is sleek, tailored, polished, and glamorous like Carolina Herrera, Emma Watson, or Charlize Theron. Your cut may have a side part or some volume and shape blown in at the roots, and your color is an iconic solid color or close to your natural one.

### The Weekend Girl

Your style is irreverent and trendy like Miley Cyrus and Rihanna. You use asymmetric angles, a shaved nape, statement color, and extreme shapes to stand out in a crowd.

# IF YOU LOVE MEDIUM-LENGTH HAIR

If you love medium-length hair, you may have a chin-length bob, a chin- to mid-neck layered shag, a bob with bangs and/or layers around the face, or a big blown-up bob with lots of volume, wave, or curl.

### The Weekend Girl

Your style is easygoing and relaxed but contemporary like Tina Fey and Jodie Foster. You work with your natural texture rather than fighting it and use mousse or thickening spray to build up body and shape.

### The Girly Girl

Your style is fashionably forward like Michelle Obama, Julianne Hough, Brooklyn Decker, Alexa Chung, and Nicole Kidman, and you like changing it up with your flat iron, curling iron, or hot rollers to vary the texture.

### The Sophisticated Girl

Your style is elegant, classy, womanly, and consistent like Adele, Oprah, Martha Stewart, Naomi Watts, Ellen Barkin, Anna Wintour, Diane Lane, and Julianna Resnick. You play with color from subtle to bold highlights to a total color statement to make your version of a bob your own.

### The Sexy Girl

You like extreme makeup and extreme color and keep switching up the volume and shape of your hair like Christina Hendricks, Paris Hilton, Nicole Richie, and Jenny McCarthy. You can never be too blond or too red.

# IF YOU LOVE LONG HAIR

If you love long hair, you may have a long collarbone-grazing bob, a shoulder-length blunt cut, long hair with layers around the face or bangs, or a true supermodel-like mane with lots of volume, wave, or curl. Long-hair girls love ponytails for a quick chic change or a fast fix for work or evening.

### The Weekend Girl

Your style is always a little windblown, wild, or bohemian like Jennifer Aniston, Kristen Stewart, Jennifer Garner, Mila Kunis, Jessica Biel, and Ashley and Mary-Kate Olsen. Even if you color it or style it, your end-result hair has an undone, free look.

### The Girly Girl

Your style is sweet but not too sweet, and you like your hair shiny and adorned with bangs, curls, swirls, and waves for a feminine effect like Zooey Deschanel, Andie MacDowell, Lucy Liu, Sarah Jessica Parker, Taylor Swift, or Reese Witherspoon.

### The Sophisticated Girl

Your style is either sculpted for a dramatic look or pulled back in a knot or ponytail like Kate Middleton, Claire Danes, Jessica Chastain, Amy Adams, or Gwyneth Paltrow. Sometimes a gel or curling iron help to achieve a waved or almost retro movie-star look.

### The Sexy Girl

Your style is extreme in size or length—ultra straight, a huge mane, or a topknot, but always attention-getting—like Kim Kardashian, Gisele Bündchen, Beyoncé, Heidi Klum, Salma Hayek, or Kate Moss.

# THE GRETTA STYLE-OVER

Rae is a cancer survivor at 24 who triumphed over lymphoma. After losing all her hair during treatment, she's reemerged with an amazing attitude and a new sophisticated style. My makeover started with Rae's hair that was a dull medium brown until I colored it a rich chestnut with cinnamon and amber highlights. I added bold bangs to frame her eyes and a completely new makeup color palette with fearless shadows and liner for a fashion forward look.

*after*

*before*

# SOURCES

p. 7 Necklace
DANNIJO Kami Necklace available at
DANNIJO.com

p. 9 Shapewear biker short
Sassy Bax by Amanda Kennedy Booty
Boosting Shaper
www.sassybax.com

p. 15 Necklace
DANNIJO Sienna Necklace available at
DANNIJO.com

p. 28 Flats
Ballet flats by Kohls
www.kohls.com

p. 28 Burgundy Leggings
Elevin Studios

p. 29 White Thin Knit
KIMBERLY OVITZ

p. 29 Orange Cardigan
Cardigan by Kohls
www.kohls.com

p. 39 Sunglasses
Courtesy of Sunglass Hut stores nationwide
www.sunglasshut.com

p. 77 Corset
Skinny Girl by Bethany Frankel Alluring
Shaping Bodysuit
www.skinnygirlshapers.com

p. 93 Nail Polish
Deborah Lippmann Nail Lacquer in
Glamorous Life (rose gold metallic) ($17)
www.DeborahLippmann.com

p. 97 Tummy Smoothing High Waist Brief
SPANX: Undie-tectable High-Waist
Shapewear Panty
www.spanx.com

p. 97 Biker Short Body Suit
Haute Contour® Sexy-Sleek Open-Bust
Mid-Thigh Body
www.spanx.com

p. 98 Control Capri Body Suit
Slim Cognito® Shape-Suit
www.spanx.com

p. 98 Butt-Boosting Shaper
Sassy Bax by Amanda Kennedy Booty
Boosting Shaper
www.sassybax.com

p. 98 Control Slip
Spanx Spoil Me Cotton Slip
www.spanx.com

p. 99 Black Control Leggings
Spanx Look at Me Cotton Leggings
www.spanx.com

p. 99 Contour Camisole
Haute Contour® Peek-a-boo Mesh
Camisole
www.spanx.com

p. 128 A New Bra in the Right Size
Full Coverage Lace Trimmed Nursing Bra
www.apeainthepod.com

p. 129 Tummy or Waist Extender
The Tummy Tube By A Pea In The
www.apeainthepod.com

p. 129 Maternity Panty
Secret Fit Shaper
www.apeainthepod.com

p. 129 Maternity Jeans
7 For All Mankind Secret Fit Belly 5 Pocket
Maternity Jeans
www.apeainthepod.com

p. 130 Long Stretch Knit Designer Maternity
Tees
Whetherly Long Sleeve Split Neck Maternity
T Shirt
www.apeainthepod.com

p. 120 Drop Yoke Yoga Pants
Splendid Fold Over Belly Jersey Knit Ruched
Maternity Yoga Pants
www.apeainthepod.com

p. 139 Clinique Take the Day Off Cleansing
Balm ($28.50)
http://www.clinique.com

p. 139 Bobbi Brown Hydrating Rich Cream
Cleanser ($28)
http://www.bobbibrowncosmetics.com/

p. 139 Neutrogena Makeup Remover
Cleansing Towelettes ($6)
http://www.neutrogena.com/

p. 139 Almay Makeup Remover Towelettes
($6)
http://www.almay.com/

p. 139 Murad Clarifying Cleanser ($26)
http://www.murad.com/

p. 139 Kate Somerville Detox Daily Cleanser
($32)
http://www.katesomerville.com/

p. 139 Peter Thomas Roth Anti-Aging
Cleansing Gel ($35)
http://www.peterthomasroth.com/

p. 139 Peter Thomas Roth Beta Hydroxy
Acid 2% Acne Wash ($ 35)
http://www.peterthomasroth.com/

p. 139 Neutrogena Naturals Acne Foaming
Scrub ($9)
http://naturals.neutrogena.com/

p. 139 Fresh Soy Face Cleanser ($38)
http://www.fresh.com/

p. 139 Clarins One-Step Exfoliating Facial
Cleanser with Orange Extract ($35)
http://int.clarins.com/

p. 139 Dior Gentle Cleansing Milk with Velvet
Peony Extract ($33)
http://www.dior.com/

p. 139 Cetaphil Daily Facial Cleanser ($12)
http://www.cetaphil.com/

p. 140 June Jacobs Perfect Pumpkin
Enzyme Polish ($60)
http://junejacobs.com/

p. 140 June Jacobs Fresh Sugar Face Polish
($55)
http://junejacobs.com/

p. 140 Peter Thomas Roth FIRMx Peeling
Gel ($48)
http://www.peterthomasroth.com/

p. 140 The Clarisonic Mia 2 ($14)
http://www.clarisonic.com/

p. 140 Shiseido Skincare Cleansing
Massage Brush ($25)
http://www.shiseido.com/

p. 140 Aveeno Positively Radiant Skin
Brightening Daily Scrub ($7)
http://www.aveeno.com/

p. 140 Simple Exfoliating Facial Wipes ($6)
http://www.simpleskincare.com/

p. 140 Simple Smoothing Facial Scrub ($7)
http://www.simpleskincare.com/

p. 140 Olay Age Defying Sensitive Skin Day Lotion SPF 15 ($12)
http://www.olay.com/

p. 140 Clinique Moisture Surge Extended Thirst Relief ($37)
http://www.clinique.com/

p. 140 By Terry Gelee de Rose Intensive Multi-Active Moisturizer ($93)
http://www.byterry.com/

p. 140 Eve Lom TLC Radiance Cream ($72)
http://www.evelom.com/

p. 140 L'Oreal Paris Youth Code Day/Night Cream Moisturizer ($25)
http://www.lorealparisusa.com/

p. 140 Boots No7 Protect & Perfect Night Cream ($25)
http://us.boots.com/

p. 140 RoC Retinol Correxion Sensitive Night Cream ($21)
http://www.rocskincare.com

p. 141 Neutrogena Ultra-Sheer Dry Touch Sunscreen SPF 45 ($8)
http://www.neutrogena.com/

p. 141 L'Oreal Paris Sublime Sun Advanced Sunscreen SPF 50 ($11)
http://www.lorealparisusa.com/

p. 141 LaRoche Posay Anthelios 50 Daily Anti-Aging Primer with Sunscreen ($40)
http://www.laroche-posay.us/

p. 141 June Jacobs Revitalizing Eye Gel ($96)
http://www.junejacobs.com/

p. 141 MAC Fast Response Eye Cream ($30)
http://www.maccosmetics.com/

p. 141 100% Pure Coffee Bean Caffeine Eye Cream ($18)
http://www.100percentpure.com/

p. 141 Olay Regenerist Eye Lifting Serum ($20)
www.olay.com

p. 141 La Mer The Eye Balm Intense ($125)
http://www.cremedelamer.com/

p. 141 Neutrogena Ageless Intensives Anti-Wrinkle Deep Wrinkle Eye ($20)
http://www.neutrogena.com/

p. 141 L'Oreal Paris Revitalift Triple Power Eye Treatment ($20)
http://www.lorealparisusa.com/

p. 142 Boots Botanics Ultra Calm Skin Relief Serum ($16)
www.boots.com

p. 142 Olay Regenerist Daily Regenerating Serum ($22)
http://www.olay.com/

p. 142 L'Oreal Paris Youth Code Youth Regenerating Skincare Serum Intense Daily Treatment ($23)
http://www.lorealparisusa.com/

p. 142 Eve Lom Intensive Hydration Serum ($95)
http://www.evelom.com/

p. 142 Boots No7 Protect & Perfect Intense Beauty Serum ($24)
http://us.boots.com/

p. 142 RoC Retinol Correxion Deep Wrinkle Serum ($21)
http://www.rocskincare.com/

p. 142 Erno Laszlo Anti-Blemish Beta Mask ($50)
http://www.ernolaszlo.com/

p. 142 Tata Harper Resurfacing Mask ($55)
http://www.tataharperskincare.com/

p. 142 Bliss That's Incredi-Peel! ($49)
http://www.blissworld.com/

p. 142 Chantecaille Detox Clay Mask ($78)
http://www.chantecaille.com/

p. 142 Freeman Facial Clay Mask with Avocado and Oatmeal ($4)
http://www.freemanbeauty.com/

p. 142 Kiss My Face Potent & Pure Pore Deep Cleansing Mask ($14)
http://www.kissmyface.com/

p. 142 Clarins Super Restorative Replenishing Comfort Mask ($62)
http://int.clarins.com/

p. 142 Darphin Youthful Radiance Camellia Mask ($70)
http://www.darphin.com/

p. 142 Freeman Feeling Beautiful Facial Enzyme Mask with Pineapple ($4)
http://www.freemanbeauty.com/

p. 142 Avene Soothing Moisture Mask ($24)
http://www.aveneusa.com/

p. 142 Burt's Bees Intense Hydration Treatment Mask ($18)
http://www.burtsbees.com/

p. 143 June Jacobs Lemon Sugar Body Polish ($48)
http://www.junejacobs.com/

p. 143 Ahava Deadsea Salt Softening Butter Salt Scrub ($24)
http://www.ahavaus.com/

p. 143 Olay Ultra Moisture Bodwash with Shea Butter ($6)
www.olay.com

p. 143 Olay Total Effects 7-in-1 Exfoliate & Replenish Bodywash ($7)
http://www.olay.com/

p. 143 CeraVe Moisturizing Lotion ($12)
http://www.cerave.com/

p. 143 Kai Body Butter ($52)
http://kaifragrance.com/

p. 143 St. Tropez Gradual Everyday Tan for the Body ($30)
http://www.sttropez.com.au/

p. 143 St. Tropez Self-Tan Mousse ($32)
http://www.sttropez.com.au/

p. 143 L'Oreal Paris Sublime Bronze Self-Tanning Towelettes for Body ($10)
http://www.lorealparisusa.com/

p. 143 Jergens Natural Glow Foaming Daily Moisturizer for the Face ($10)
http://www.jergens.com

p. 151 Cle de Peau Beaute Concealer ($70)
http://www.cledepeau-beaute.com/

p. 151 Lancôme Effacernes Waterproof Under-Eye Concealer ($30)
http://www.lancome-usa.com/

p. 151 L'Oreal Paris True Match Super-Blendable Crayon Concealer ($9)
http://www.lorealparisusa.com/

p. 151 Trish McEvoy Flawless Concealer ($38)
http://www.trishmcevoy.com/

p. 151 Neutrogena Healthy Skin Brightening Eye Perfector ($13)
http://www.neutrogena.com/

p. 151 Smashbox Camera Ready BB Cream SPF 35 ($39)
http://www.smashbox.com/

p. 151 Stila All Day 10-in-1 HD Beauty Balm with Broad Spectrum SPF 30 ($38)
http://www.stilacosmetics.com/

p. 151 Too Faced Air Buffed BB Complete Coverage Makeup Broad Spectrum Sunscreen SPF 20 ($39)
http://www.sephora.com/

p. 151 Clinique Age Defense BB Cream Broad Spectrum SPF 30 ($37)
www.clinique.com

p. 151 Bobbi Brown BB Cream Broad Spectrum SPF 30 ($42)
http://www.bobbibrowncosmetics.com/

p. 151 L'Oreal Paris Age Perfect BB Cream SPF 20 ($17)
http://www.lorealparisusa.com/

p. 152 Smashbox Studio Skin 15-Hour Wear Foundation ($42)
http://www.smashbox.com/

p. 152 Too Faced BB Creme Complete Nars Matte Oil-Free Foundation ($44)
http://www.sephora.com/

p. 152 Chantecaille Future Skin Foundation ($72)
http://www.chantecaille.com/

p. 152 Neutrogena SkinClearing Oil-Free Makeup ($14)
http://www.neutrogena.com/

p. 152 Dior Beauty AirFlash Spray Foundation ($62)
http://www.dior.com/

p. 152 Armani Beauty Designer Cream Foundation SPF 20 ($65)
http://www.giorgioarmanibeauty-usa.com/

p. 152 Becca Radiant Skin Satin Finish Foundation ($42)
http://www.beccacosmetics.com/

p. 152 Revlon Nearly Naked Makeup SPF 20 ($10)
http://www.revlon.com/

p. 152 Revlon ColorStay Whipped Crème Makeup ($14)
http://www.revlon.com/

p. 152 L'Oreal Paris Visible Lift Repair Absolute Rapid Age Reversing Makeup ($15)
http://www.lorealparisusa.com/

p. 152 L'Oreal Paris True Match Lumi Healthy Luminous Makeup SPF 20
http://www.lorealparisusa.com/

p. 153 Smashbox Brow Tech ($25)
http://www.smashbox.com/

p. 153 DiorShow Brow Styler ($29)
http://www.dior.com/

p. 153 Trish McEvoy Precision Brow Shaper ($28)
http://www.trishmcevoy.com/

p. 153 Sephora Eyebrow Editor Complete Brow Kit ($19)
http://www.sephora.com/

p. 153 Tweezerman Slant Tweezer ($25)
http://www.tweezerman.com/

p. 153 Tweezerman Point Tip Tweezer ($23)
http://www.tweezerman.com/

p. 153 Maybelline Fit Me! Blush ($6)
http://www.maybelline.com/

p. 153 NARS The Multiple ($39)
http://www.narscosmetics.com/

p. 153 Stila Convertible Color ($25)
http://www.stilacosmetics.com/

p. 153 Armani Sheer Blush ($44)
http://www.giorgioarmanibeauty-usa.com/

p. 153 By Terry Velvet Cream Blush ($44)
http://www.byterry.com/

p. 153 Maybelline Dream Bouncy Blush ($8)
http://www.maybelline.com/

p. 153 L'Oreal Paris Visible Lift Color Lift Blush ($13)
http://www.lorealparisusa.com/

p. 153 Dior Beauty Airflash Spray Foundation ($62)
http://www.dior.com/

p. 153 Armani Designer Shaping Cream Foundation SPF 20 ($65)
http://www.giorgioarmanibeauty-usa.com/

p. 153 Becca Radiant Skin Satin Finish Foundation ($42)
http://www.beccacosmetics.com/

p. 153 Revlon Nearly Naked Makeup SPF 20 ($10)
http://www.revlon.com/

p. 153 Revlon ColorStay Whipped Creme Makeup ($14)
http://www.revlon.com/

p. 153 L'Oreal Paris Visible Lift Repair Absolute Rapid Age Reversing Makeup ($15)
http://www.lorealparisusa.com/

p. 153 L'Oreal Paris True Match Lumi Healthy Luminous Makeup SPF 20 ($13)
http://www.lorealparisusa.com/

p. 154 Tarte LipSurgence Lip Tint ($24)
http://tartecosmetics.com/

p. 154 Yves Saint Laurent Rouge Pur Couture Vernis A Lèvres Glossy Stain ($34)
http://www.yslbeautyus.com/

p. 154 Fresh Sugar Tinted Lip Treatment ($22.50)
http://www.fresh.com/

p. 154 Clinique Chubby Stick Intense Moisturizing Lip Colour Balm ($16)
http://www.clinique.com/

p. 154 Stila Color Balm Lipstick ($22)
http://www.stilacosmetics.com/

p. 154 Revlon ColorBurst Lip Butter ($7)
http://www.revlon.com/

p. 154 L'Oreal Colour Riche Caresse Wet Shine Stain ($10)
http://www.lorealparisusa.com/

p. 154 Illamasqua Bronzing Duo ($34)
http://www.illamasqua.com

p. 154 Diorskin Nude Tan Healthy Glow Enhancing Powder ($55)
http://www.dior.com

p. 154 Physicians Formula Bronze Booster Glow Boosting Pressed Bronzer ($15)
http://www.physiciansformula.com

p. 154 Iman Sheer Finish Bronzing Powder ($16)
http://www.imancosmetics.com

p. 154 Urban Decay 24/7 Glide-On Eye Pencil ($19)
http://www.urbandecay.com/

p. 154 Maybelline Unstoppable Eyeliner ($6)
http://www.maybelline.com/

p. 155 Urban Decay Naked 2 Palette ($50)
http://www.urbandecay.com/

p. 155 Stila in the Know Eye Shadow Palette ($39)
http://www.stilacosmetics.com

p. 155 Tarte Call of The Wild Amazonian Clay 8-Shadow Collector's Palette ($36)
http://www.tartecosmetics.com/

p. 155 Lorac Unzipped ($40)
http://www.loraccosmetics.com

p. 155 Smashbox Photo Op Eye Enhancing Palette ($39)
http://www.smashbox.com/

p. 155 Maybelline ExpertWear Quad Eyeshadow ($5),
http://www.maybelline.com

p. 155 Maybelline EyeStudio Eyeshadow Quad ($10),
http://www.maybelline.com

p. 155 Wet n Wild Color Icon Collection Eyeshadow Trio ($3)
http://wnwbeauty.com/

p. 155 Shu Uemura Eyelash Curler ($20)
http://www.shuuemura-usa.com/Eyelash-Curler

p. 155 Le Métier de Beauté Curler ($18)
http://www.lemetierdebeaute.com/

p. 155 L'Oreal Paris Voluminous Mascara ($9)
http://www.lorealparisusa.com

p. 155 Dior Diorshow Black Out Mascara ($25)
http://www.dior.com/Diorshow

p. 155 Ardell Fashion Lashes ($4)
http://www.ardelllashes.com/

p. 155 Andrea Modlash ($4)
www.madamemadeline.com/

p. 163 Kerastase Mask Elixir Ultime ($65)
http://www.kerastase-usa.com/

p. 163 Davines Glorifying Anti-age Shimmering Pak ($35)
http://www.davines.com/

p. 163 Kiehl's Since 1851 Superbly Smoothing Argan Hair Pak ($25)
http://www.kiehls.com/

p. 163 Living Proof Restore Mask Treatment ($42)
http://www.livingproof.com

p. 163 Phytocitrus Color Protect Radiance Mask ($39)
http://www.phyto-usa.com/

p. 163 Carol's Daughter Monoi Repairing Hair Mask ($29)
http://www.carolsdaughter.com

p. 163 Organix Ever Straight Brazilian Keratin Therapy Hydrating Keratin Masque ($7)
http://www.organixhair.com/

p. 163 L'Oreal Paris Advanced Haircare Total Repair 5 Damage Erasing Balm ($7)
http:// www.lorealparisusa.com

p. 163 Garnier Fructis Haircare Sleek & Shine Moroccan Sleek Oil Treatment ($6)
http:// www.garnierusa.com/

p. 163 L'Oreal Paris Kerastase Reflection Bain Chroma Captive ($39)
www.kerastase-usa.com/

p. 163 Lait Richesse Conditioner ($41)
http://www.kerastase-usa.com

p. 163 L'Oreal Paris Color Vibrancy Nourishing Shampoo ($5) and Conditioner ($5)
http://www.lorealparisusa.com/

p. 163 Kerastase Bain Volumactive ($39)
http://www.kerastase-usa.com/

p. 163 Lait Volumactive ($41)
http://www.kerastase-usa.com/

p. 163 Nexxus Hydra Light Weightless Moisture Shampoo ($11) and Conditioner ($16)
http:// www.nexxus.com/

p. 163 Kerastase Bain Force Architecte ($39)
http://www.kerastase-usa.com/

p. 163 Ciment Anti-Usure ($41)
http://www.kerastase-usa.com/

p. 163 Organix Anti-Breakage Keratin Oil Shampoo ($8)
http://www. www.organixhair.com/

p. 163 Organix Smooth Hydration Argan Oil & Shea Butter Conditioner ($8)
http://www. www.organixhair.com/

p. 164 Mason Pearson Handy Mix Hair Brush and paddle ($120)
http://www.masonpearson.com/

p. 164 Marilyn Tuxedo Pro brush ($23)
http:// www.themarilynbrush.com/

p. 164 Oscar Blandi Pronto Dry Styling Heat Protect Spray ($23)
http://www.oscarblandi.com

p. 164 John Frieda Frizz Ease Heat Defeat Protective Styling Spray ($6)
www.johnfrieda.com/FrizzEase

p. 164 Tresemme Keratin Smooth Heat Style Spray (6$)
http://www.tresemme.com/

p. 164 John Frieda Frizz-Ease Thermal Protection Serum ($9)
http://www.johnfrieda.com/

p. 164 Nexxus Heat Protexx Heat Protection Styling Spray ($11)
http:// www.nexxus.com/

p. 165 T3 Featherweight Journey Travel Dryer ($130)
http://www.t3micro.com/

p. 165 T3 Featherweight 2 ($200)
http://www.t3micro.com/

p. 165 Hot Tools 12-Piece Tourmaline Professional Hairsetter ($36)
http://www.hottools.com/

p. 165 John Frieda Smooth Waves Hairsetter ($40)
www.johnfrieda.com/

p. 165 Oscar Blandi Pronto Texture & Volume Spray ($25)
http://www.oscarblandi.com/

p. 165 L'Oreal Paris EverStyle Texture Series Energizing Dry Shampoo ($7)
http://www.lorealparisusa.com/

p. 165 John Frieda Luxurious Volume All-Day Volume Refresher ($7)
http://www.johnfrieda.com/

p. 165 HairUWear Simply Straight Pony Extension ($40)
http://www.hairuwear.com/

p. 165 Goody Thick Ponytail Elastics ($5)
http://www.goody.com/

p. 165 Goody Simple Styles Spin Pin ($6)
http://www.goody.com/

p. 166 The T3 SinglePass Professional Straightening and Styling Iron ($160)
http://www.t3micro.com/irons/

p. 166 Hot Tools 1.5 inch Ceramic Tourmaline Curling Iron ($35)
www.hottools.com/

p. 166 Oribe Volumista Mist for Volume ($38)
www.oribe.com/

p. 166 Alterna Bamboo Volume 48-Hour Sustainable Volume Spray ($25)
www.alternahaircare.com/

p. 166 Redken Guts 10 Volume Spray Foam ($17)
www.redken.com

p. 166 Josie Maran Argan Oil Hair Serum ($30)
www.josiemarancosmetics.com/hair

p. 166 Phytodefrisant Botanical Straightening Balm ($28)
www.sephora.com

p. 166 L'Oreal Paris Smooth Intense Frizz Taming Serum ($7)
www.lorealparisusa.com

p. 166 Ojon Super Sleek Restorative Blowout Perfector ($25)
www.ojon.com

p. 166 Ouidad Curl Quencher Hydrafusion Intense Curl Cream ($22)
www.ouidad.com/

p. 166 Redken Body Full Carbo-Bodifier Volumizing Foam ($18)
www.redken.com

p. 166 John Frieda Frizz-Ease Curl Reviver Styling Mousse for Curly Styles ($6)
www.johnfrieda.com/FrizzEase

# PHOTO CREDITS

iii **Aunt Kathy and Gretta**
courtesy of the author

iv **Kelly Ripa**
Getty Images/Dimitrios Kambouris

iv **Beyonce Knowles; Oprah Winfrey**
Getty Images/Larry Busacca

iv **Erica Hill**
Getty Images/Astrid Stawiarz

iv **Carrie Keagan**
Getty Images/Jamie McCarthy

iv **Giuliana Rancic**
Getty Images/Gilbert Carrasquillo

iv **Maria Menounos**
Getty Images/Dave Kotinsky

iv **Katie Couric**
Getty Images/**Kevin** Mazur

iv **Lara Spencer**
Getty Images/Raymond Hall

iv **Sherri Shepherd**
Getty Images/Daniel Zuchnik

iv **Tamara Mowry; Tia Mowry**
Getty Images/ Jeff Kravitz

iv **Beth Ostrosky Stern**
Getty Images/Dimitrios Kambouris

iv **Daphne Oz**
Getty Images/ David Livingston

iv **Ali Wentworth**
Getty Images/Robin Marchant

iv **Wendy Williams**
Getty Images/Bravo

1–4 Family photos
courtesy of the author

7 **Lipstick, varied colors** (top left)
by Media Bakery

7 **Stiletto pumps** (top right)
by Media Bakery

7 **Signature necklace** (bottom left)
by Media Bakery

7 **Dark stretch jeans** (bottom right)
by Media Bakery

8 **Black bra** (top left)
by Media Bakery

8 **Olivia Wilde** (top right)
by Larry Busacca/Getty Images

8 **Tailored jacket** (bottom left)
by Media Bakery

8 **Gabrielle Union** (bottom right)
by Astrid Stawiarz/Getty Images

9 **Nude laser-cut bike short** (top)
photography by Jack Deutsch

9 **Diane Lane** (bottom)
by Lester Cohen/Getty Images

13 **Sunglasses** (top left)
by Media Bakery

13 **Kerry Washington** (upper middle)
by Jamie McCarthy/Getty Images

13 **Beach bag** (upper middle)
by Media Bakery

13 **Hat** (top right)
by Media Bakery

13 **Espadrilles** (top right)
by Media Bakery

13 **Cameron Diaz** (middle left)
by Arnaldo Magnani/Getty Images

13 **Bobbi Brown** (center)
by Slaven Vlasic/ Getty Images

13 **Keira Knightly** (center)
by Venturelli/Getty Images

13 **Olivia Munn** (middle right)
by Alberto E. Rodriguez/Getty Images

13 **Blonde in sunglasses** (bottom middle)
by Media Bakery

13 **Maxi dress** (bottom right)
by Media Bakery

15 **Pink shoes** (top left)
by Media Bakery

15 **Lacy top on chair** (top left)
by Media Bakery

15 **Brooke Burke-Charvet** (top center)
by Paul A. Hebert/Getty Images

15 **Half leg** (top right)
by Media Bakery

15 **White top** (top right)
by Media Bakery

15 **Reese Witherspoon** (middle left)
by Chris Jackson/Getty Images

15 **Emmy Rossum** (middle left)
by Chelsea Lauren/Getty Images

15 **Taylor Swift** (center)
by Ray Tamarra/Getty Images

15 **Emma Stone** (middle right)
by Jemal Countess/Getty Images

15 **Pink tights/purple shoes** (far right)
by Media Bakery

15 **Kelly Bensimon** (bottom left)
by Theo Wargo/Getty Images

15 **Kate Bosworth** (bottom left)
by Frazer Harrison/Getty Images

15 **Girl in skirt** (middle)
by Media Bakery

15 **Girl in hood** (bottom right)
by Media Bakery

15 **Necklace** (bottom right)
by DANNIJO Kami

15 **Chanel** (bottom center)
by Media Bakery

17 **Blonde in glasses** (top left)
by Media Bakery

17 **Pearls with gloves** (top left)
by Media Bakery

17 **Olivia Palmero** (top left)
by Ben Pruchnie/Getty Images

17 **Diane Sawyer** (top center)
by Kris Connor/ Getty Images

17 **Queen Latifah** (top right)
by Handout/Getty Images

17 **Angelina Jolie** (top right)
by James Devaney/Getty Images

17 **Louise Roe** (middle left)
by Ray Tamarra/Getty Images

17 **Nina Garcia** (center)
by Rob Kim/Getty Images

17 **Laughing girl** (center)
by Media Bakery

17 **Kali Hawk** (middle right)
by Jon Kopaloff/Getty Images

17 **Hoda Kotb** (bottom left)
by Gary Gershoff/Getty Images

17 **Black boots** (bottom middle)
by Media Bakery

17 **Red shoes** (bottom left)
by Media Bakery

17 **Black patent bag** (bottom left)
by Media Bakery

17 **Mila Kunis** (bottom right)
by Pascal Le Segretain/Getty Images

17 **Anna Wintour** (bottom right)
by Bertrand Rindoff Petroff/Getty Images

17 **Kate Middleton** (bottom right)
Max Mumby/Indigo/Getty Images

19 **Anja Rubik** (top left)
by Getty Images/ Dominique Charriau

19 **Rihanna** (top left)
by Steve Granitz/Getty Images

19 **Jennifer Lopez shoes** (top middle)
by Jason Merritt/Getty Images

19 **Leopard print** (top middle)
by Media Bakery

19 **Heeled boots** (top right)
by Media Bakery

19 **Jennifer Lopez in leopard print** (top right)
by Alo Ceballos/Getty Images

19 **Gwyneth Paltrow** (middle left)
by Carlos Alvarez/Getty Images

19 **Girl in silver** (bottom left)
by Media Bakery

19 **Bustier** (center)
by Media Bakery

19 **Jennifer Hudson** (bottom right)
by James Devaney/Getty Images

19 **Eva Longoria** (bottom right)
by Marc Piasecki/Getty Images

19 **Kelsey Chow** (bottom center)
by Lester Cohen/Getty Images

19 **Snakeskin clutch** (bottom left)
by Media Bakery

25 **Style-Over**
Photography by Gail Hadani

28 **Pewter flats** (top)
by Kohls

28 **Burgundy leggings** (bottom)
by Elevin Studios

29 **Plain white knit** (top left)
by Kimberly Ovitz

29 **Printed top** (top right)
by Dimitrios Kambouris/Getty Images

29 **Orange Cardigan** (bottom left)
by Kohls

29 **Sarah Jessica Parker** (bottom right)
by Ray Tamarra/Getty Images

30 **Kate Middleton** (top left)
by Max Mumby/Indigo/Getty Images

30 **Anne Hathaway** (top right)
by VP/Star Max/Getty Images

30 **Ray Bans** (bottom left)
by Sunglass Hut

30 **Handbag** (bottom right)
by Yigal Azruoel

32 **Jessica Alba** (left)
by JB Lacroix/Getty Images

32 **Cameron Diaz** (right)
by Arnaldo Magnani/Getty Images

33 **Carmen Electra** (left)
by Alexandra Wyman/Getty Images

33 **Taylor Swift** (right)
by JB Lacroix/Getty Images

34 **Kristen Stewart** (left)
by Lester Cohen/Getty Images

34 **Mila Kunis** (right)
Pascal Le Segretain/Getty Images

35 **Blake Lively** (left)
by James Devaney/Getty Images

35 **Eva Mendes** (right)
by Arnaldo Magnani/Getty Images

40 **Louise Roe**
by Ray Tamarra/Getty Images

41 **Emma Stone**
by Jemal Countess/ Getty Images

42 **Kelly Bensimon**
by Theo Wargo/Getty Images

43 **Kerry Washington**
by Jamie McCarthy/Getty Images

44 **Miranda Kerr**
by Jason LaVeris/Getty Images

45 **Style-Over**
Photography by Gail Hadani

48 **Robin Roberts**
by Steve Mack / Getty Images

49 **Pumps on running model** (left)
by Media Bakery

49 **Angelina Jolie** (right)
by James Devaney / Getty Images

50 **Queen Latifah** (left)
by Frederick M. Brown / Getty Images

50 **Olivia Palmero** (right)
by Jason Kempin/Getty Images

51 **Olivia Wilde** (left)
by Alo Ceballos/ Getty Images

51 **Katie Lee** (top right)
51 **Bethenny Frankel** (bottom right)
by Alo Ceballos/Getty Images

52 **Nina Garcia** (left)
by Rob Kim/Getty Images

52 **Olivia Palmero** (right)
by Ray Tamarra/Getty Images

54 **Gretta/Tim**
by Bravo

58 **Ashley Roberts** (left)
by Ben Pruchnie/Getty Images

58 **Bobbi Brown** (right)
by Slaven Vlasic/Getty Images

59 **Taylor Swift** (left)
by Ray Tamarra/Getty Images

59 **Zoe Saldana** (right)
by Frazer Harrison/Getty Images

60 **Anna Wintour** (left)
by Bertrand Rindoff Petroff/Getty Images

60 **Hoda Kotb** (right)
by Gary Gershoff/Getty Images

61 **Olivia Wilde** (left)
by Ray Tamarra/Getty Images

61 **Tamara Mellon** (right)
by Jamie McCarthy/Getty Images

62 **Style-Over**
Photography by Gail Hadani

65 **Jennifer Hudson** (top)
by James Devaney/Getty Images

65 **Gwyneth Paltrow** (bottom)
by Carlos Alvarez/Getty Images

66 **Brooke Burke** (top left)
by Paul A. Hebert/Getty Images

66 **Diane Sawyer** (top right)
by Kris Connor/Getty Images

66 **Hilary Swank** (bottom left)
by Julien Hekimian/Getty Images

66 **Jennifer Aniston** (bottom right)
by Ray Tamarra/Getty Images

67 **Cameron Richardson** (top left)
by Joe Kohen/Getty Images

67 **Naomi Watts** (top right)
by Gregg DeGuire/Getty Images

67 **Hilary Swank** (bottom left)
by Venturelli/Getty Images

67 **Rosie Huntington-Whiteley** (bottom right)
by Paul Archuleta/Getty Images

70 **Sarah Hyland** (left)
by Ben Gabbe/ Getty Images

70 **Olivia Munn** (right)
by Alberto E. Rodriguez/Getty Images

71 **Danielle Jonas** (left)
by Matthew Eisman/Getty Images

71 **Zooey Deschanel** (right)
by Michael Buckner/Getty Images

72 **Kristen Bell** (left)
by Christopher Polk/Getty Images

72 **Kali Hawk** (right)
by Jon Kopaloff/Getty Images

73 **Nicky Hilton** (left)
by Jennifer Graylock/Getty Images

73 **Eva Longoria** (right)
by Marc Piasecki/Getty Images

76 **Balcony Bra** (far left)
by Media Bakery

76 **Push-up bra** (middle)
by Media Bakery

76 **Thongs and Bra** (far right)
by Media Bakery

77 **Demi-Brief** (far left)
by Media Bakery

77 **Fishnets** (left middle)
by Media Bakery

77 **Corset** (right middle)
by Media Bakery

78 **Style-Over**
Photography by Gail Hadani

81 **Zoe Saldana** (top)
by Josiah Kamau/Getty Images

81 **Kelly Rowland** (bottom)
by Frederick M. Brown/Getty Images

82 **White blouse** (top left)
by Media Bakery

82 **Brooke Burke-Charvet** (top right)
by Michael Tran/Getty Images

82 **Jordana Brewster** (bottom left)
by Jon Kopaloff/Getty Images

82 **Eva Longoria** (bottom right)
by Buzzfoto/Getty Images

83 **Zoe Saldana Handbag** (top left)
by Josiah Kamau/Getty Images

83 **Kerry Washington** (top right)
by Dave M. Benett/Getty Images

83 **Jane Fonda** (bottom left)
by Frazer Harrison/Getty Images

83 **Zoe Saldana** (bottom right)
by Josiah Kamau/Getty Images

86 **Padma Lakshmi** (left)
by  Ben Gabbe/Getty Images

86 **Keira Knightly** (right)
by Venturelli/Getty Images

87 **Katy Perry** (left)
by Christopher Polk/Getty Images

87 **Pippa Middeton** (right)
by Alo Ceballos/Getty Images

88 **Stacy Keibler** (left)
by Jennifer Graylock/Getty Images

88 **Anne Hathaway** (right)
by Jason Kempin/Getty Images

89 **Lisa Rinna** (left)
by Bruce Glikas/Getty Images

89 **Beyonce** (right)
by Kevin Mazur/Getty Images

92 **Katie Lee shoe** (left)
by Michael Kovac/Getty Images

92 **Cocktail ring** (middle)
by Media Bakery

92 **Chanel bag** (right)
by Venturelli/Getty Images

# ACKNOWLEDGMENTS

## Thank you to my personal gotta-haves

*Style and the Successful Girl* was made possible by the love, faith, and encouragement of my family, friends, and colleagues.

**THANK YOU** to my Boston Besties : ) Nicole, Katie, and Andrea for all the talks, tears, laughter, loyalty, and honest interventions.

**THANK YOU** to my Boston Blood : ) Aunts Emily, Elaine, Lenore, Suzi, and Casey for endless cheers, love, and last-minute babysitting.

**THANK YOU** to my Hometown Heroes my work "family" : ) Team Grettacole, Gretta Luxe, and Gspa for sharing your amazing talent, hard work, long hours, and devotion to our clients and community. You make every one of our clients feel special and beautiful and me feel humbled, grateful, and proud every day.

**THANK YOU** to the Fearless Females who make things happen : )

Rachael Ray for feeding, teaching, and inspiring me

To Katie Lee, for becoming family, being my sister, and for being there for me through it all

June Jacobs for bringing me back to NYC, and for all you have given me in work and family. I love you.

Lois Joy Johnson for your dedication to my story, daily counseling and tolerance of my 2 a.m. panic emails. You made this book better than I could've ever imagined—we are friends for life.

**THANK YOU** to the men who inspire me and bring joy and fulfillment into my life

My dearest Kai, you are my heart and the greatest gift of my lifetime

Ricky, the love of my life . . . for your spirit, patience, and love and for making my life beautiful and complete

Uncle Ed, for stepping up to be my dad, for your hugs, kisses, and Oreos

Tim Gunn, my work husband, my friend, and guru for life